8 Practice Tests
for
Reading and Math

Grade 4

by Michael Priestley

New York • Toronto • London • Auckland • Sydney •
Mexico City • New Delhi • Hong Kong • Buenos Aires

Scholastic Inc. grants teachers permission to photocopy the designated reproducible pages from this book for classroom use. No other part of this publication may be reproduced in whole or in part, or stored in a retrieval system, or transmitted in any form or by any means electronic, mechanical, photocopying, recording or otherwise, without written permission of the publisher. For information regarding permission, write to Scholastic Inc., 555 Broadway, New York, NY 10012.

Cover design by Kelli Thompson
Interior design by Creative Pages Inc.
Interior illustrations by Kate Flanagan

ISBN 0-439-33818-2

Copyright © 2002 by Michael W. Priestley. All rights reserved.
Printed in the U.S.A.

Contents

Introduction

In this book, you will find eight Practice Tests designed to help your students prepare to take standardized tests. Each Practice Test has two parts—Reading and Math. Each test part has 20–30 multiple-choice items that closely resemble the kinds of questions students will have to answer on "real" tests. Each part of the test will take 30–40 minutes for students to complete.

The Reading and Math skills measured in these tests and the types of questions are based on detailed analyses and correlations of the five most widely used standardized tests and the curriculum standards measured by many statewide tests, including the following:

Stanford Achievement Test	California's STAR Test
CTBS TerraNova	TAAS (Texas)
Metropolitan Achievement Test	MCAS (Massachusetts)
Iowa Test of Basic Skills	FCAT (Florida)
California Achievement Test	New York

How to Use the Tests

To use a Practice Test, make a copy of the test or part of the test for each student. Tell students how much time they will have to complete the test. Encourage students to work quickly and carefully and to keep track of the remaining time—just as they would in a real testing session. You may have students mark their answers directly on the test pages, or you may have them use a copy of the **Answer Sheet** on page 87. The answer sheet may be used with any of the Practice Tests, and it will help students become accustomed to filling in bubbles on a separate answer sheet. It may also make the tests easier for you to score.

For the Math section in each test, we do not recommend the use of calculators. For Practice Tests 2 and 6, students will need an inch ruler and a centimeter ruler to answer some of the questions.

At the back of this book, you will find **Tested Skills** charts and **Answer Keys** for the eight Practice Tests. The Tested Skills charts list the skills measured in each test and the test questions that measure each skill. These charts may be helpful to you in determining what kinds of questions your students answered incorrectly, what skills they may be having trouble with, and who may need further instruction in particular skills. To score a Practice Test, refer to the Answer Key for that test. The Answer Key lists the correct response to each question.

To score a Practice Test, go through the test and mark each question answered correctly. Add the total number of questions answered correctly to find the student's test score. To find a percentage score, divide the number correctly answered by the total number of questions. For example, the percentage score for a student who answers 20 out of 25 Reading questions correctly is $20 \div 25 = 0.80$, or 80%. In your classroom, you might want to have students correct their own tests. This will give students a chance to see where they made mistakes and what they need to do to improve their scores on the next test.

On the next two pages of this book, you will find **Test-Taking Tips** for Reading and Math. You may want to share these tips and strategies with students before they begin working on the Practice Tests. You may also want to post these tips in the classroom and discuss them when students are preparing to take tests.

Test-Taking Tips: Reading

1. For each part of the test, read the directions carefully so you know what to do. Then read the directions again—just to make sure.

2. For questions about a reading passage, take a quick look at the questions first. Then you will know what to look for as you read the passage.

3. In each question, look for key words to help you decide what the question is asking. Examples of key words: *who, what, when, where, how, why.*

4. You do not have to memorize the information in each passage before you answer the questions. Go back to the passage to find the answers you need.

5. To find the sequence of events, look for signal words, such as *first, last, then, next, before, after, later, finally.* You may also look for numbers, such as years or dates.

6. To figure out the meaning of an unfamiliar word in a passage, look for clues in the sentence. Be sure to look in the sentences before and after the word, too.

7. To find causes and effects, look for signal words and phrases, such as *because, so, since, as a result.*

8. When answering a question, read all the answer choices carefully. Consider each possible answer before you choose one.

9. To find the main idea of a passage, decide what the whole passage is mostly about. Use the title and any pictures on the page to help you figure it out.

10. Be on the lookout for negative words in questions or directions, such as *not, opposite, except, unless.* These words may be in all CAPITAL letters, in **bold** type or *italics*, or underlined. Questions using these words can be confusing. Think carefully about what the question is asking before you choose an answer.

Test-Taking Tips: Mathematics

1. For each part of the test, read the directions carefully so you know what to do. Then read the directions again—just to make sure.

2. Look for key words and phrases to help you decide what each question is asking and what kind of computation you need to do. Examples of key words: *less than, greatest, least, farther, longest, divided equally.*

3. To help solve a problem, write a number sentence or equation.

4. Use scrap paper (or extra space on the test page) to write down the numbers and information you need to solve a problem.

5. If a question has a picture or diagram, study it carefully. Draw your own picture or diagram if it will help you solve a problem.

6. Try to solve each problem before you look at the answer choices. (In some tests, the correct answer may be "Not Given" or "Not Here," so you will want to be sure of your answer. In these Practice Tests, some of the Math questions use "NG" for "Not Given.")

7. Check your work carefully before you finish. (In many questions, you can check your answer by working backwards to see if the numbers work out correctly.)

8. If you are not sure which answer is correct, cross out every answer that you know is wrong. Then make your best guess.

9. To complete a number sentence or equation, try all the answer choices until you find the one that works.

10. When working with fractions, always reduce (or rename) the fractions to their lowest parts. When working with decimals, keep the decimal points lined up correctly.

Practice Test 1
Reading
Directions. Choose the meaning of the underlined word. Mark your answer.

1. To <u>chuckle</u> is to —
- Ⓐ work
- Ⓑ laugh
- Ⓒ listen
- Ⓓ forget

2. A <u>cactus</u> is a kind of —
- Ⓕ boat
- Ⓖ sound
- Ⓗ cloth
- Ⓙ plant

3. A <u>diagram</u> is a kind of —
- Ⓐ building
- Ⓑ tree
- Ⓒ tool
- Ⓓ drawing

4. To <u>observe</u> means to —
- Ⓕ eat
- Ⓖ watch
- Ⓗ return
- Ⓙ take

5. A <u>response</u> is —
- Ⓐ an officer
- Ⓑ a present
- Ⓒ an answer
- Ⓓ a cover

6. Something that is <u>wobbly</u> is —
- Ⓕ shaky
- Ⓖ gentle
- Ⓗ flat
- Ⓙ shiny

7. <u>Fortunate</u> means —
- Ⓐ afraid
- Ⓑ friendly
- Ⓒ lucky
- Ⓓ sudden

8. To <u>imitate</u> means to —
- Ⓕ copy
- Ⓖ change
- Ⓗ pay
- Ⓙ help

9. Something that is <u>thrilling</u> is —
- Ⓐ helpful
- Ⓑ damp
- Ⓒ exciting
- Ⓓ small

10. <u>Hastily</u> means —
- Ⓕ quickly
- Ⓖ sweetly
- Ⓗ bravely
- Ⓙ carefully

11. A <u>blunder</u> is —
- Ⓐ a reward
- Ⓑ a mistake
- Ⓒ an enemy
- Ⓓ a memory

12. To <u>seize</u> means to —
- Ⓕ fall
- Ⓖ shine
- Ⓗ sip
- Ⓙ grab

GO ON ⟩

Practice Test 1 *(continued)*

Directions. Read each passage. Choose the best answer to each question. Mark your answer.

New Neighbors

A moving van arrived at the house next door. Ben looked out the window and saw a friendly-looking man directing the movers where to put the boxes and furniture. Ben ran over and said, "I'm Ben. I live next door."

"I'm Mr. Tull," the friendly-looking man replied.

"Do you have any kids my age?" asked Ben.

With a laugh, Mr. Tull said, "Mrs. Tull will arrive tonight with Jesse, our ten-year-old." Then he added, "I saw the basketball hoop in your driveway. Jesse loves basketball."

Ben hurried home to give Mom a report about the Tulls. "They have a boy my age, and he loves basketball!" he exclaimed.

The next morning, Ben heard a knock on the door. Then he heard Mom say, "Well, hello, Jesse Tull. It's nice to meet you." Grabbing his basketball, Ben scurried to the door to meet Jesse. When he saw a girl with brown pigtails, Ben's jaw dropped open.

"I'm Jesse," said the girl, smiling. "Would you like to play basketball?"

"But you're a —" Ben began. Then he laughed and said, "Sure, let's go!"

13. **What do you think will happen next?**
- Ⓐ Jesse will go back home.
- Ⓑ Ben and Jesse will meet some other friends.
- Ⓒ Ben will help Jesse unpack.
- Ⓓ Ben and Jesse will play basketball.

14. **What happened just after Ben met Mr. Tull?**
- Ⓕ Ben told his mom about the Tulls.
- Ⓖ A moving van arrived.
- Ⓗ Ben grabbed his basketball.
- Ⓙ Ben met Jesse.

15. **How did Ben feel when he first met Jesse?**
- Ⓐ shy
- Ⓑ surprised
- Ⓒ bored
- Ⓓ afraid

16. **This story is most like a —**
- Ⓕ fable
- Ⓖ tall tale
- Ⓗ true story
- Ⓙ play

GO ON ▷

Practice Test 1 *(continued)*

Almost There

Word spread quickly through the crowded passenger compartment. *We've reached New York Harbor!* As everyone began moving up the stairs to the ship's deck, Mama held Maria's hand firmly. "Stay right beside me," Mama said.

A few minutes later, they were standing on the deck. "Oh, Maria," Mama exclaimed. "I can see the Statue of Liberty, and it's just as beautiful as Papa said!"

"Lift me up, Mama!" cried Maria. "I want to see it, too!"

Mama grunted as she lifted Maria. Both mother and daughter felt weak from having eaten so little during their three-week voyage, but the sight of the beautiful statue gave them strength.

Then Mama noticed an island with a large brick building. "That must be Ellis Island," she said. "Papa told me about it in his last letter. He said we'll get off there, and the people in charge will check to make sure we're healthy. They'll ask where we've come from and how we'll manage to get by here in America."

Maria's back stiffened with pride. "You'll tell them Papa has been here for a year and has a good job in a shoe factory, and an apartment waiting for us, too."

"Yes, Maria, that's what I'll say," smiled Mama. "Won't it be wonderful to see Papa after all this time?"

Closing her eyes, Maria could clearly picture Papa's smiling face. She tried to picture her new street, her new home, and her new friends, but those things were harder to see in her mind. "I'll just have to wait," Maria told herself, "but it won't be long now!"

17. Where are Maria and Mama?
- Ⓐ on an island
- Ⓑ in an apartment
- Ⓒ on a ship
- Ⓓ in a brick building

18. When they see the Statue of Liberty, Maria and her mother feel —
- Ⓕ sad
- Ⓖ afraid
- Ⓗ lonely
- Ⓙ excited

19. How does Papa know about Ellis Island?
- Ⓐ He works there.
- Ⓑ He read about it in a book.
- Ⓒ He stopped there when he arrived.
- Ⓓ He heard about it from friends.

20. Which of these can Maria picture most easily?
- Ⓕ her new apartment
- Ⓖ the friends she will make
- Ⓗ her father's face
- Ⓙ her new street

Practice Test 1 *(continued)*

The Three Wishes

Long ago, a husband and wife had a farm where they worked long and hard each day. They scarcely had enough to eat, but they lived happily enough. The husband took pleasant walks after supper with his dog, while his wife tended her rose garden.

One day, as the husband and wife were working in their field, they heard a voice crying out for help. Looking up, they a saw a tiny man who had fallen into a nearby creek. "I can't swim!" cried the man. "Save me!"

The husband and wife ran to the creek and pulled the tiny man out. Grateful for their help, he said, "To thank you for saving me, I will grant you three wishes." Then with a quick bow, the tiny man disappeared.

"Shall we make our wishes now?" asked the husband.

"Let's finish our day's work and make our wishes after supper," said his wife. "That will give us time to think about what we want most."

So the husband and wife kept working until the sun set, imagining the grand house, fine clothes, and bags of gold that might soon be theirs. When they finally went inside for supper, the wife began preparing their usual meal of soup and bread, but the husband was very hungry. Without thinking he declared, "How I wish we could have roast beef for supper!"

As soon as the husband spoke, a platter of roast beef appeared on the table.

"Oh, no!" cried the wife. "You've wasted a wish on a single meal!"

"I'm sorry," the husband said, "but we still have two wishes left. If we use them wisely, two will be enough."

The wife wasn't listening, though, for just then she looked out the window and saw that her husband's dog was trampling her roses. "That useless dog!" she exclaimed. "I wish he'd never been born!"

As soon as she spoke, the dog began to shrink and shrink until he was gone.

"Look what you've done!" cried the man. "What will I do without my dog?"

The woman embraced her husband. "I'm so sorry," she said, "I should have thought before I spoke." Then she smiled brightly and said, "We still have one wish left. Let's use it to make everything right again."

The husband took his wife's hands in his, smiled, and nodded.

Practice Test 1 *(continued)*

21. What do you think the husband and wife will do next?

    Ⓐ They will look for the tiny man.

    Ⓑ They will pick some roses from the garden.

    Ⓒ They will eat their roast beef dinner.

    Ⓓ They will make a wish to get the dog back.

22. The boxes show some events from the story.

1	2	3
A tiny man fell into the creek.		The wife began preparing soup and bread.

Which of these should go in Box 2?

    Ⓕ The tiny man granted the husband and wife three wishes.

    Ⓖ A platter of roast beef appeared on the table.

    Ⓗ The husband's dog trampled the wife's roses.

    Ⓙ The wife wished the dog had never been born.

23. What can you tell about the tiny man?

    Ⓐ He was wicked.

    Ⓑ He liked to swim.

    Ⓒ He was rich.

    Ⓓ He had magic powers.

24. Which of these was most important to the husband?

    Ⓕ a grand house

    Ⓖ bags of gold

    Ⓗ fine clothes

    Ⓙ his dog

25. What can you tell about the woman in this story?

    Ⓐ She was unhappy most of the time.

    Ⓑ She was a good cook.

    Ⓒ She cared about her husband's feelings.

    Ⓓ She was a lazy worker.

26. What lesson does this story teach?

    Ⓕ Don't work too hard.

    Ⓖ Be happy with what you have.

    Ⓗ Everyone needs good luck.

    Ⓙ Never help a stranger in need.

Name _____ Date _____

Practice Test 1
𝕸athematics

Directions. Choose the best answer to each question. Mark your answer.

1. The Dent Bridge in Idaho is 1050 feet long. Which words mean 1050?
- Ⓐ ten thousand fifty
- Ⓑ ten thousand five
- Ⓒ one thousand fifty
- Ⓓ one hundred fifty

2. What goes in the box to make this number sentence true?

$6 \times 4 = \Box$

- Ⓕ $6 + 4$
- Ⓖ 4×6
- Ⓗ $6 - 4$
- Ⓙ $6 + 6 + 6 + 6 + 6 + 6$

3. Which river is longest?

Majors Rivers of Asia	
Name	**Length (miles)**
Chang	3964
Ganges	1560
Huang	3395
Lena	2734
Ob	2268

- Ⓐ Huang
- Ⓑ Chang
- Ⓒ Lena
- Ⓓ Ob

4. What fractional part of this figure is shaded?

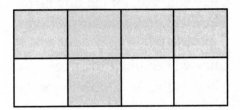

- Ⓕ $\frac{1}{4}$
- Ⓗ $\frac{3}{8}$
- Ⓖ $\frac{3}{5}$
- Ⓙ $\frac{5}{8}$

5. Which number is equal to $(6 \times 1000) + (4 \times 100) + (5 \times 1)$?
- Ⓐ 645
- Ⓒ 6405
- Ⓑ 6045
- Ⓓ 6450

6. Tim has a lemonade stand. The chart shows how much lemonade he sold each day.

Day	Lemonade Sold
Wednesday	$\frac{1}{4}$ gallon
Thursday	$\frac{2}{3}$ gallon
Friday	$\frac{1}{6}$ gallon
Saturday	$\frac{3}{4}$ gallon

On which day did Tim sell the most lemonade?
- Ⓕ Wednesday
- Ⓗ Friday
- Ⓖ Thursday
- Ⓙ Saturday

GO ON

Practice Test 1 *(continued)*

7. Which address is an odd number?
- Ⓐ 96 Cole Road
- Ⓑ 48 Main Street
- Ⓒ 20 Brook Road
- Ⓓ 73 Pine Street

8. Which figure shows $\frac{2}{3}$ shaded?

Ⓕ   Ⓗ

Ⓖ   Ⓙ

9. This table shows the number of games won by the Hornets hockey team each year.

Year	1998	1999	2000	2001	2002
Games Won	2	5	8	11	

If this pattern continues, what number should go in the box for 2002?
- Ⓐ 15
- Ⓑ 14
- Ⓒ 13
- Ⓓ 12

This chart lists the highest mountain in each of the six New England states. Use it to answer questions 10 and 11.

Mountains of New England		
State	**Mountain**	**Elevation (feet)**
Connecticut	Frissell	2380
Maine	Katahdin	5267
Massachusetts	Greylock	3487
New Hampshire	Washington	6288
Rhode Island	Jerimoth Hill	812
Vermont	Mansfield	4393

10. The highest mountain is in which state?
- Ⓕ Connecticut
- Ⓖ Maine
- Ⓗ Massachusetts
- Ⓙ New Hampshire

11. Which mountain is taller than Jerimoth Hill but shorter than Greylock?
- Ⓐ Frissell
- Ⓑ Katahdin
- Ⓒ Washington
- Ⓓ Mansfield

GO ON ⇨

Practice Test 1 *(continued)*

12. Mr. Barnes drove his truck 4237 miles. What is that number rounded to the nearest hundred?

- Ⓕ 4000
- Ⓖ 4200
- Ⓗ 4300
- Ⓙ 5000

13. Claire earned $587 last month. What is that amount rounded to the nearest ten?

- Ⓐ $500
- Ⓑ $580
- Ⓒ $590
- Ⓓ $600

14. What goes in the box to make the number sentence true?

$$(3 + 8) + 10 = 3 + (\square + 10)$$

- Ⓕ 6
- Ⓖ 7
- Ⓗ 8
- Ⓙ 10

15. A birthday card costs $1.85. <u>About</u> how much would 300 cards cost?

- Ⓐ $30–$40
- Ⓑ $50–$60
- Ⓒ $300–$400
- Ⓓ $500–$600

16. Which number sentence is correct?

- Ⓕ $6 \times 0 = 0$
- Ⓖ $6 + 0 = 0$
- Ⓗ $6 \times 1 = 6 + 1$
- Ⓙ $0 \times 6 = 6 \times 1$

17. Sam made this pattern of shapes.

If the pattern continues, what shape should come next?

- Ⓐ ◯
- Ⓑ △
- Ⓒ ●
- Ⓓ ▲

GO ON

Practice Test 1 (continued)

18. Which pair of numbers are factors of 42?

- Ⓕ 4, 8
- Ⓖ 5, 15
- Ⓗ 6, 7
- Ⓙ 9, 13

19. The population of Newton is four thousand thirty-five. Which number means four thousand thirty-five?

- Ⓐ 4035
- Ⓑ 4305
- Ⓒ 4350
- Ⓓ 40,035

20. Which sign shows an even number?

- Ⓕ | Route I-95 |
- Ⓖ | 15 Avenue |
- Ⓗ | 27 Street |
- Ⓙ | Route 128 |

21. What number is equal to $(8 \times 1000) + (7 \times 100) + (2 \times 10)$?

- Ⓐ 80,720
- Ⓑ 8720
- Ⓒ 8702
- Ⓓ 8072

22. Randy was thinking of a number with a 9 in the hundreds place. Which of these could be the number?

- Ⓕ 5290
- Ⓖ 1925
- Ⓗ 9137
- Ⓙ 2409

23. A total of 7324 people went to the county fair on Saturday, and 4191 people went to the fair on Sunday. Which numbers would give the best estimate of the total number of people at the fair for both days?

- Ⓐ 8000 + 4000
- Ⓑ 8000 + 5000
- Ⓒ 7000 + 5000
- Ⓓ 7000 + 4000

GO ON ⟩

Practice Test 1 *(continued)*

24. Which number sentence goes with
12 − 5 = 7?

- Ⓕ 7 − 5 = 2
- Ⓖ 12 + 5 = 17
- Ⓗ 12 + 7 = 19
- Ⓙ 5 + 7 = 12

25. Millie put a total of 465 marbles in
3 boxes. There are 220 marbles in
Box 1 and 55 marbles in Box 2. How
many marbles are in Box 3?

- Ⓐ 175
- Ⓑ 190
- Ⓒ 275
- Ⓓ 290

26. Last year, the population of Elton was
12,420. Since then, the population has
grown by 160 people. Which number
sentence should be used to find the
total population of Elton now?

- Ⓕ 12,420 × 160 = ☐
- Ⓖ 12,420 − 160 = ☐
- Ⓗ 12,420 + 160 = ☐
- Ⓙ 12,420 ÷ 160 = ☐

27. Mr. Clooney sells men's hats. The table
shows 4 hats and the size of each hat.

Hat	Size (inches)
1	$7\frac{1}{2}$
2	$8\frac{1}{4}$
3	$6\frac{3}{4}$
4	$7\frac{3}{8}$

Which is the largest hat?
- Ⓐ Hat 1
- Ⓑ Hat 2
- Ⓒ Hat 3
- Ⓓ Hat 4

28. Which figure shows forty-five
hundredths shaded?

Ⓕ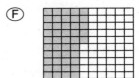

Ⓖ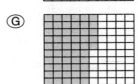

Ⓗ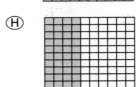

Ⓙ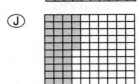

STOP

Practice Test 2
Reading

Directions. Read the sentence in the box. Choose the answer in which the underlined word has the same meaning. Mark your answer.

1.
> Will you please scratch my <u>back</u>?

In which sentence does <u>back</u> have the same meaning?

(A) Jan has a sunburn on her <u>back</u>.
(B) I sat in the <u>back</u> of the room.
(C) Take three steps <u>back</u>.
(D) The boys ran <u>back</u> to the house.

2.
> Joe gets <u>cross</u> when he's tired.

In which sentence does <u>cross</u> have the same meaning?

(F) I'll <u>cross</u> your name off the list.
(G) Why is Mom so <u>cross</u> with you?
(H) You can <u>cross</u> the road now.
(J) <u>Cross</u> your fingers for good luck.

3.
> Henry ate the <u>last</u> piece of cake.

In which sentence does <u>last</u> have the same meaning?

(A) I had a great dream <u>last</u> night.
(B) The peace and quiet didn't <u>last</u>.
(C) Kim used the <u>last</u> sheet of paper.
(D) How long did your lesson <u>last</u>?

4.
> Is it time to <u>stop</u> working?

In which sentence does <u>stop</u> have the same meaning?

(F) Let's <u>stop</u> at the library.
(G) Please <u>stop</u> talking now.
(H) I'll meet you at the bus <u>stop</u>.
(J) Use the plug to <u>stop</u> up the drain.

5.
> Today is the first day of <u>fall</u>.

In which sentence does <u>fall</u> have the same meaning?

(A) My tooth is ready to <u>fall</u> out.
(B) Lucy took a <u>fall</u> and hurt herself.
(C) Vinnie visits us every <u>fall</u>.
(D) Darkness will <u>fall</u> in an hour.

6.
> Turn on the bedroom <u>light</u>.

In which sentence does <u>light</u> have the same meaning?

(F) Bina will <u>light</u> the candles.
(G) Is that box heavy or <u>light</u>?
(H) Dad's jacket is <u>light</u> blue.
(J) That <u>light</u> needs a new bulb.

GO ON

Practice Test 2 *(continued)*

Directions. Read each passage. Choose the best answer to each question. Mark your answer.

ℌarry or ⅅorothy?

What do you think is the best children's story ever written? Today, many people would choose *Harry Potter and the Sorcerer's Stone*. Before Harry Potter showed up, *The Wonderful Wizard of Oz* was probably the best-loved children's story of all time. A man named L. Frank Baum wrote the story about 100 years ago. *The Wizard of Oz* movie was made in 1939. It has been seen by more people than any other movie ever made.

In some ways, these two stories are alike. Each story tells about a child who has an adventure—Dorothy in *The Wizard of Oz* and Harry Potter. Each story is a fantasy that involves magic. Dorothy has magical silver slippers (which were changed to ruby red in the movie). Harry has a magic wand and magical spells. Both stories have struggles between good and evil. Dorothy has to face the <u>wicked</u> witch. Harry has to face an evil wizard named Voldemort. All in all, both stories are quite wonderful.

7. The passage says, "Dorothy has to face the <u>wicked</u> witch." The word <u>wicked</u> means —
- (A) pretty
- (B) evil
- (C) lonely
- (D) dark

8. In what way are *The Wizard of Oz* and *Harry Potter* stories alike?
- (F) Both were written at the same time.
- (G) Both involve silver slippers.
- (H) Both are about young boys.
- (J) Both tell about a child's adventure.

9. Which sentence is an opinion?
- (A) Each story tells about a child.
- (B) *The Wizard of Oz* movie was made in 1939.
- (C) Both stories are quite wonderful.
- (D) L. Frank Baum wrote *The Wonderful Wizard of Oz*.

10. Which is another good title for this passage?
- (F) "Great Children's Stories"
- (G) "The Life of L. Frank Baum"
- (H) "The Wicked Witch"
- (J) "Magical Silver Slippers"

Practice Test 2 *(continued)*

A Page from Carli's Journal

Lately Dena's been copying everything I do! Last week I got a new pair of sneakers (which I really needed because my old ones were worn out). I picked out white sneakers with yellow and green stripes, and I liked them because no one else had a pair like them. Then yesterday, Dena came to school with the exact same sneakers! If that were the only thing she copied, I wouldn't mind, but she copied my new haircut and made herself a bead bracelet just like mine, too!

I must have let on how annoyed I was, because Mrs. Hale called me to her desk after recess. "You seem upset, Carli," she said. When I told her about Dena, she made an interesting point. She thinks Dena copies me because I'm kind of a leader in our class. "The other kids respect you, Carli," said Mrs. Hale.

Then Mrs. Hale gave me some advice. She said Dena needs to feel more <u>confident</u> about herself. "Try to notice a choice Dena makes by herself, and say something nice about it," Mrs. Hale suggested. "Then she won't feel the need to copy you so much."

So today, when Dena rode her bike to school, I told her I liked riding my bike to school, too. You should have seen the smile on Dena's face! Now she and I are going to start riding our bikes to school together.

I hope Mrs. Hale's suggestion will help me stay friends with Dena.

11. This page from Carli's journal is mostly about —
- (A) what she likes to wear
- (B) her problem with Dena
- (C) the kids in her class
- (D) her new haircut

12. Why did Carli buy new sneakers?
- (F) Her old ones were too small.
- (G) She wanted an extra pair.
- (H) Her old ones were worn out.
- (J) She wanted a pair like Dena's.

13. How is Carli different from Dena?
- (A) She can't ride a bike.
- (B) She makes things with beads.
- (C) She is a class leader.
- (D) She copies other girls.

14. The passage says, "Dena needs to feel more <u>confident</u>." What does <u>confident</u> mean?
- (F) sure of herself
- (G) worried
- (H) surprised by others
- (J) sorry

15. Carli followed Mrs. Hale's advice because she wanted to —
- (A) make some new friends
- (B) pretend that Dena didn't bother her
- (C) show that she respected Mrs. Hale
- (D) stay friends with Dena

Practice Test 2 *(continued)*

A Safe Place to Play

One day a boy named Bobby Adams was playing in the street near his home in Davie, Florida, when he was hit by a car. Bobby was not injured badly, but his friend, nine-year-old James Ale, got angry. James wasn't angry at Bobby for playing in the street. He wasn't even angry at the driver of the car. He was angry at his town government. Why? Bobby, James, and their friends played in the street because there was no place else nearby to play. While kids in other parts of Davie played safely in neighborhood parks, the town wouldn't spend money to build a park for James's neighborhood. His neighborhood was a nice place to live, but it wasn't safe to play there.

James Ale decided to change that. He wrote a petition that said his neighborhood needed a park. Then he asked his friends to sign it. Most of them laughed at James, claiming that no one would ever pay attention to kids.

However, James was just getting started. He made an appointment with the mayor. Then he took a town map and marked the location where a park for his neighborhood could be built. He also wrote a letter that explained the need for the park. He listed items the park should have, such as a basketball court, swings, and monkey bars.

On the day of his appointment, James dressed in his best clothes. He put his map and his letter in a briefcase and walked into the mayor's office. Calmly and politely, James made his case for the neighborhood park. Mayor Joan Kovac listened carefully. Then she shared James's idea with other town officials, but they didn't show much interest in it.

Still James persisted. A newspaper reporter from Miami wrote an article about James's plan for a neighborhood park, and James sent a copy of the article to the town officials. Every few days, he called Mayor Kovac to make sure she didn't forget about him. Finally, James got some great news. At a town meeting, the mayor announced plans to build the neighborhood park.

These days, the kids in James's neighborhood have a safe place to play, thanks to a young boy who refused to take no for an answer. James had a good idea, and he never gave up. Today, the park that he fought long and hard for is known as "James Ale Park."

Practice Test 2 *(continued)*

16. What is this passage mainly about?
- (F) why Bobby and James became friends
- (G) what James Ale did to get a park for his neighborhood
- (H) what kinds of things should be in a park
- (J) how a person gets to be mayor of a town

17. When Bobby Adams was hit by a car, James got angry at —
- (A) Bobby
- (B) the driver of the car
- (C) a newspaper reporter
- (D) his town government

18. Compared with James's neighborhood, the other neighborhoods in town were —
- (F) safer
- (G) bigger
- (H) noisier
- (J) cleaner

19. Why do you think James wore his best clothes to the meeting with Mayor Kovac?
- (A) He wanted her to take him seriously.
- (B) His other clothes were dirty.
- (C) He was playing a dress-up game.
- (D) He thought his picture would be in the newspaper.

20. Which detail supports the idea that James was well prepared for his meeting with the mayor?
- (F) He got angry at his town's government.
- (G) He called the mayor's office.
- (H) He thought his neighborhood was a nice place to live.
- (J) He got a town map and marked the location for the park.

21. The passage says, "Still James persisted." What does persisted mean?
- (A) stayed safe
- (B) got worried
- (C) kept trying
- (D) became angry

22. Which sentence states an opinion?
- (F) James asked his friends to sign the petition.
- (G) His neighborhood was a nice place to live.
- (H) James marked a location for the park on a town map.
- (J) Every few days James called Mayor Kovac.

Name _____ Date _____

Practice Test 2
𝔐athematics
Directions. Choose the best answer to each question. Mark your answer.

1. Which is a rectangle?

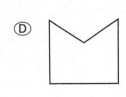

2. Which figure has exactly 4 faces?

Use the street map below to answer questions 3 and 4.

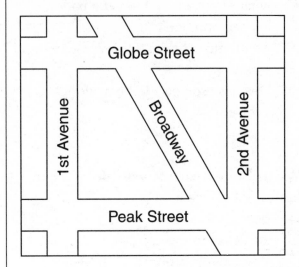

3. Which two streets appear to be parallel?
- Ⓐ 1st Avenue and Peak Street
- Ⓑ Globe Street and Peak Street
- Ⓒ 1st Avenue and Broadway
- Ⓓ Globe Street and 2nd Avenue

4. Which street does *not* intersect with 2nd Avenue?
- Ⓕ 1st Avenue
- Ⓖ Globe Street
- Ⓗ Broadway
- Ⓙ Peak Street

GO ON

Practice Test 2 (continued)

5. Suppose that each figure can be folded on the dotted line. In which figure are the two parts exactly the same?

Ⓐ

Ⓒ

Ⓑ

Ⓓ

6. This box will be turned on its side, as shown by the arrow.

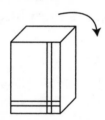

Which picture shows the box turned on its side?

Ⓕ

Ⓗ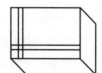

Ⓖ

Ⓙ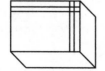

7. Kerry has a rectangular yard for her dogs.

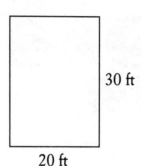

30 ft

20 ft

What is the perimeter of the yard?
Ⓐ 600 ft
Ⓑ 100 ft
Ⓒ 80 ft
Ⓓ 50 ft

8. This picture shows the tiles on Martin's kitchen floor. Each tile is 1 square foot. What is the area of the floor?

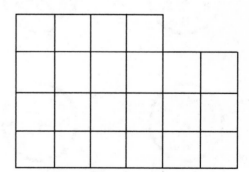

Ⓕ 18 sq ft
Ⓖ 20 sq ft
Ⓗ 22 sq ft
Ⓙ 24 sq ft

GO ON

Practice Test 2 *(continued)*

9. Rico found these coins in his pocket. What is the value of the coins?

- Ⓐ $0.33
- Ⓑ $0.63
- Ⓒ $0.68
- Ⓓ $0.73

10. Stella woke up at 6:25 A.M. Which clock shows the time she woke up?

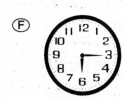 

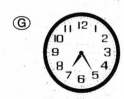 

11. The clock below shows the time when Tomás put a pie in the oven to bake. The pie was done 1 hour 15 minutes later. What time was the pie done?

12:30

- Ⓐ 12:45
- Ⓑ 1:30
- Ⓒ 1:45
- Ⓓ 2:00

12. A family car is most likely to be which length?
- Ⓕ 20 inches
- Ⓖ 20 feet
- Ⓗ 20 yards
- Ⓙ 20 miles

13. Which unit should be used to measure the amount of water in a backyard swimming pool?
- Ⓐ gallons
- Ⓑ pounds
- Ⓒ feet
- Ⓓ ounces

GO ON ⇨

Practice Test 2 (continued)

14. This map shows a secret path through the park. What is the length of the path on the map? (Use an inch ruler.)

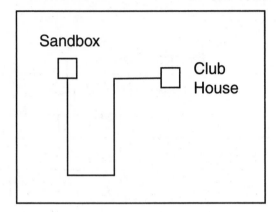

(F) $1\frac{1}{2}$ in.   (H) $2\frac{1}{2}$ in.

(G) 2 in.   (J) 3 in.

15. How long is the butterfly pin from wing to wing? (Use a centimeter ruler.)

(A) 4 cm
(B) 5 cm
(C) 6 cm
(D) 7 cm

16. What temperature is shown on the thermometer?

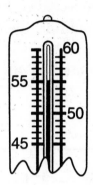

(F) 45°F
(G) 50°F
(H) 55°F
(J) 60°F

17. Mrs. Dolan drove her taxi 285 miles on Monday, 390 miles on Tuesday, and 205 miles on Wednesday. **About** how far did she drive all together?

(A) 600 miles
(B) 700 miles
(C) 800 miles
(D) 900 miles

18. Chet earns from $36 to $43 per week on his paper route. **About** how much does he earn in 4 weeks?

(F) $180
(G) $160
(H) $140
(J) $120

GO ON

Practice Test 2 *(continued)*

A 4th-grade class is collecting money for a field trip. This bar graph shows how much money the students collected each week. Use the graph to answer questions 19 and 20.

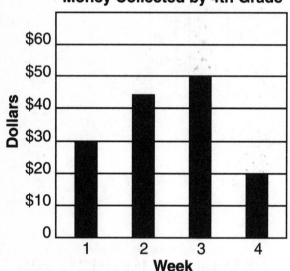

Money Collected by 4th Grade

19. In which week did students collect the most money?

ⓐ Week 1
ⓑ Week 2
ⓒ Week 3
ⓓ Week 4

20. How much more did students collect in Week 2 than in Week 4?

ⓕ $45
ⓖ $25
ⓗ $15
ⓙ $10

Shannon took a survey of 4th graders. She asked students to choose their favorite foods. She made a tally chart to show the results of the survey. Use the chart to answer questions 21 and 22.

Favorite Foods

Mac & Cheese	卌 卌 卌 卌 I
Pizza	卌 卌 IIII
Spaghetti	卌 卌 卌 II
Tacos	卌 卌 卌 卌 III
Hamburger	卌 卌 I

21. Which food was chosen by the greatest number of students?

ⓐ Mac & Cheese
ⓑ Pizza
ⓒ Spaghetti
ⓓ Tacos

22. How many students chose spaghetti?

ⓕ 17
ⓖ 18
ⓗ 21
ⓙ 23

STOP

Practice Test 3
Reading

Directions. Read each sentence and find the meaning of the underlined word. Mark your answer.

1. Our dog <u>irritated</u> all the neighbors by barking most of the night. The word <u>irritated</u> means —

   Ⓐ noticed
   Ⓑ amused
   Ⓒ helped
   Ⓓ bothered

2. Did the doctor figure out what kind of <u>ailment</u> you have? <u>Ailment</u> means —

   Ⓕ sickness
   Ⓖ work
   Ⓗ talent
   Ⓙ time

3. Rita was <u>reluctant</u> to try out for the school play until her friends talked her into it. <u>Reluctant</u> means —

   Ⓐ expected
   Ⓑ happy
   Ⓒ ready
   Ⓓ unwilling

4. To <u>summon</u> the police or the fire department, dial 911. <u>Summon</u> means —

   Ⓕ write
   Ⓖ thank
   Ⓗ call
   Ⓙ join

5. I've read the directions twice, but I still can't <u>comprehend</u> them. The word <u>comprehend</u> means —

   Ⓐ understand
   Ⓑ see
   Ⓒ return
   Ⓓ fix

6. The boys found a <u>reasonable</u> way to share the chores, so everyone was happy. <u>Reasonable</u> means —

   Ⓕ boring
   Ⓖ fancy
   Ⓗ fair
   Ⓙ strange

7. The wagon will gain <u>velocity</u> as it heads down the hill. The word <u>velocity</u> means —

   Ⓐ size
   Ⓑ speed
   Ⓒ passengers
   Ⓓ wheels

8. The <u>humorous</u> story made everyone laugh. <u>Humorous</u> means —

   Ⓕ long
   Ⓖ funny
   Ⓗ true
   Ⓙ frightening

GO ON

Practice Test 3 *(continued)*

Directions. Read each passage. Choose the best answer to each question. Mark your answer.

Dad's Rules

Dad pushed the cart past the long check-out lines and steered into the express lane. "We have more than ten items," said Sandy. "We can't use the express."

"We're only a few over," answered Dad, "and we're in a rush. I'm sure this nice lady won't mind." Dad put a bag of potatoes on the counter and smiled at the clerk. She didn't smile back.

On the drive home, Dad anxiously checked his watch. Sandy checked the speedometer. "Hey, Dad," she said, "the speed limit here is 35 miles an hour, and you're going 45!"

"Relax, Sandy," Dad answered. "There's hardly any traffic, and I'm a good driver."

At home, Dad and Sandy put the groceries away. Then Dad turned on the oven and started peeling potatoes. Sandy turned on the TV and started watching.

"Hey, Sandy," Dad called, "no TV before homework. You know the rules!"

"You know the rules, too," Sandy replied. "But you used the express lane, and you were speeding on the way home."

Dad was about to scold Sandy for being fresh, but he stopped and thought for a minute. "You know, you're right, Sandy," he said. "I'll try to set a better example. Now get going on your homework."

9. The "express lane" in this story is —
Ⓐ on a highway
Ⓑ in a supermarket
Ⓒ at a theater
Ⓓ in a fast-food restaurant

10. What will probably happen next?
Ⓕ Dad will go for a drive.
Ⓖ Sandy will make dinner.
Ⓗ Dad will watch TV.
Ⓙ Sandy will do her homework.

11. Dad broke rules in this story because he —
Ⓐ didn't know any better
Ⓑ is a careless person
Ⓒ was in a big hurry
Ⓓ doesn't believe in rules

12. This story suggests that —
Ⓕ it is wrong to point out a parent's mistake
Ⓖ following rules is always easy
Ⓗ children often behave the way their parents do
Ⓙ most rules aren't important

Practice Test 3 *(continued)*

The Rainmaker

Everyone in Cedar Valley knew the instant Junior was born. When he started bawling, the sound was like thunder. Ma, Pa, and the other folks clapped their hands over their ears and ran for cover until Junior cried himself to sleep. Before long, the valley folks told Ma and Pa to head for the hills. "And stay there till that boy learns to lower his voice!" they said.

So Ma and Pa packed up Junior and moved away to Blue Mountain. As he grew, Junior bawled less and talked more, but his words were as thunderous as his cries. Ma and Pa gave up trying to teach Junior to speak softly. Instead they took to plugging their ears with beeswax.

In time, folks in the valley darned near forgot about Ma, Pa, and Junior— until the summer when the rain never fell. The river dried up, and so did the crops. Storm clouds sometimes drifted by, but not a drop of rain fell. "We need to get those clouds to open up," the valley folks said, "but how?"

Then the valley folks remembered Junior. The next time storm clouds drifted by, they journeyed up to Blue Mountain. "Come to the valley and give a yell," they begged Junior.

So Junior left the mountain for the first time and stood under the storm clouds in the valley. Then he cupped his hands to his mouth and yelled. Sure enough, the storm clouds started rolling around like giant water balloons. When they collided, they burst open and showered the valley till the river was flowing and the crops were growing again.

Of course, Junior was a hero, so nobody wanted to send him back up to Blue Mountain. That's why all the folks in Cedar Valley started plugging their ears with beeswax.

13. What kind of story is this?
- Ⓐ a fairy tale
- Ⓑ a biography
- Ⓒ a tall tale
- Ⓓ a science fiction story

14. What happened soon after Junior was born?
- Ⓕ Ma, Pa, and Junior moved away.
- Ⓖ The storm clouds burst open.
- Ⓗ Folks plugged their ears with beeswax.
- Ⓙ Crops started growing again.

15. How did folks feel about Junior at the end of the story?
- Ⓐ angry
- Ⓒ afraid
- Ⓑ grateful
- Ⓓ puzzled

16. What lesson does this story teach?
- Ⓕ Some people should live alone.
- Ⓖ Babies cause lots of trouble.
- Ⓗ Everyone has a special talent.
- Ⓙ Don't cry over little things.

Practice Test 3 *(continued)*

On Shaky Ground

Mom held the door open as Fluffy took a few cautious steps onto the porch. He let out a low growl and hurried back inside. "I don't know what's up with your cat, Pam," Mom sighed as she sat down for breakfast. "He's refused to go out all morning."

"Maybe Mr. Grady's dog is loose in the neighborhood again," I suggested.

Just then my Wheaty-O's started dancing in my bowl, and Mom's teacup jiggled in its saucer. The dining room pictures were tapping against the walls, and in the living room, a book tumbled from the bookcase.

In a split second, Mom and I were standing under the doorframe between the kitchen and the dining room. "Nathan!" Mom shouted. "Where are you?"

Just then the bathroom door swung open, and Dad ran out and joined us. He was wearing his bathrobe, and his face was covered with shaving cream. We stood with our arms around one another, wondering if the shaking would get worse. It didn't. In fact, in less than a minute, it stopped. We waited about two minutes more just to be sure. Then we all breathed a sigh of relief.

Before long, Mr. Grady was knocking on the door. "Everyone okay in there?" he wanted to know.

"No harm done," Dad said as Mr. Grady stepped inside. "That wasn't much of a quake."

"Can't be too sure about that, of course," Mr. Grady said. "That little shake could be a warning that a bigger earthquake's coming. My dog seems to think so, anyway. He's been hiding under my bed all morning."

"Funny, that's where our cat has been most of the morning, too," said Mom.

Mr. Grady had a point, but we'd all been through this before, and we knew that even the earthquake experts didn't know what would happen next. Getting on with the day and keeping our fingers crossed were the only things we could do.

Practice Test 3 *(continued)*

17. **What do you think will happen next?**
- Ⓐ Mr. Grady will make his dog go outside.
- Ⓑ Pam will get ready for bed.
- Ⓒ Dad will finish shaving.
- Ⓓ Mom will call an earthquake expert.

18. **These boxes show some events from the story.**

1	2	3
Fluffy hurried inside.		Mom shouted for Dad.

Which of these best fits in Box 2?
- Ⓕ Mr. Grady knocked on the door.
- Ⓖ Mom's teacup started jiggling.
- Ⓗ The shaking stopped.
- Ⓙ Dad ran out of the bathroom.

19. **You can tell from this story that when an earthquake starts, it is a good idea to —**
- Ⓐ go to a basement
- Ⓑ stand on a porch
- Ⓒ go to an attic
- Ⓓ stand under a doorframe

20. **What is the mood of this story?**
- Ⓕ funny
- Ⓖ suspenseful
- Ⓗ peaceful
- Ⓙ sad

21. **This story suggests that animals —**
- Ⓐ cause problems when danger strikes
- Ⓑ are braver than humans
- Ⓒ usually don't know how to protect themselves
- Ⓓ can often sense danger before humans do

22. **What does this story suggest about earthquakes?**
- Ⓕ They are hard to predict.
- Ⓖ They happen in every part of the world.
- Ⓗ They always last several minutes.
- Ⓙ They usually cause a lot of damage.

Practice Test 3
𝔐athematics
Directions. Choose the best answer to each question. Mark your answer. If the correct answer is *not given,* choose "NG."

1. On Saturday, 73 people went to the two o'clock movie at the theater. Each person paid $4.00. How much money did the theater collect in all?
Ⓐ $332.00
Ⓑ $292.00
Ⓒ $146.00
Ⓓ $18.25
Ⓔ NG

2. A total of 84 students are going on a field trip to the science museum. If 8 students can ride in each van, which number sentence should you use to find the number of vans needed for the field trip?
Ⓕ $84 + 8 = \Box$
Ⓖ $84 - 8 = \Box$
Ⓗ $84 \times 8 = \Box$
Ⓙ $84 \div 8 = \Box$
Ⓚ NG

3. Mrs. Carver made 345 sandwiches for the school picnic. Students ate 286 of the sandwiches. How many sandwiches were left?
Ⓐ 41
Ⓑ 55
Ⓒ 59
Ⓓ 69
Ⓔ NG

4. Jeremy uses 6 beads to make a dream catcher. How many dream catchers can he make with 92 beads?
Ⓕ 12
Ⓖ 14
Ⓗ 15
Ⓙ 16
Ⓚ NG

5. Amanda jogged 4.9 miles on Monday and 7.3 miles on Wednesday. How many miles did she jog in all?
Ⓐ 2.4 miles
Ⓑ 3.6 miles
Ⓒ 11.2 miles
Ⓓ 12.4 miles
Ⓔ NG

GO ON

Practice Test 3 *(continued)*

6. Robbie bought this jacket in a department store. He gave the clerk a $20.00 bill.

$16.95

How much change should Robbie get back?

- Ⓕ $2.95
- Ⓖ $3.05
- Ⓗ $3.15
- Ⓙ $4.05
- Ⓚ NG

7. Selena was 4 ft 10 in. last year. Since then she has grown 3 inches. How tall is she now?

- Ⓐ 4 ft 7 in.
- Ⓑ 4 ft 11 in.
- Ⓒ 5 ft 2 in.
- Ⓓ 5 ft 3 in.
- Ⓔ NG

8. Bilbo has these marbles in his collection.

Bilbo's Marbles	
Cat's eye	105
Aggies	62
Glass	47

How many marbles does he have in all?

- Ⓕ 104
- Ⓖ 114
- Ⓗ 204
- Ⓙ 214
- Ⓚ NG

9. Mr. Breen bought $1\frac{1}{2}$ pounds of cake flour and $2\frac{1}{2}$ pounds of bread flour. How much flour did he buy all together?

Cake Flour $1\frac{1}{2}$ lb   Bread Flour $2\frac{1}{2}$ lb

- Ⓐ 3 lb
- Ⓑ $3\frac{1}{2}$ lb
- Ⓒ 4 lb
- Ⓓ $4\frac{1}{2}$ lb
- Ⓔ NG

GO ON

Practice Test 3 *(continued)*

10. Git works 28 hours each week. He worked 7 hours on Monday and 6 hours on Tuesday. How many more hours does he have to work this week?

Ⓕ 41
Ⓖ 22
Ⓗ 21
Ⓙ 15
Ⓚ NG

11. Nina fell asleep on the sofa at 4:15 P.M. She woke up at 5:45 P.M. How long did she sleep?

Ⓐ 1 hr 15 min
Ⓑ 1 hr 30 min
Ⓒ 1 hr 45 min
Ⓓ 2 hr
Ⓔ NG

12. Lance rode his bicycle across the United States. The trip took 64 days. How many weeks did the trip last?

Ⓕ 6 weeks 4 days
Ⓖ 8 weeks 6 days
Ⓗ 9 weeks 1 day
Ⓙ 10 weeks
Ⓚ NG

13. A puppy named Max weighs 12 pounds. Max gains 2 pounds per week. At this rate, how much will Max weigh in 3 weeks?

Ⓐ 14 lb
Ⓑ 15 lb
Ⓒ 17 lb
Ⓓ 18 lb
Ⓔ NG

14. Clem scored 34 points in a basketball game. Leo scored 26 points. Which number sentence should you use to find how many more points Clem scored?

Ⓕ $26 + 34 = \square$
Ⓖ $26 - 34 = \square$
Ⓗ $34 \times 26 = \square$
Ⓙ $34 \div 26 = \square$
Ⓚ NG

15. Buzzy started watching a video at 9:30 A.M. The video lasted 80 minutes. At what time did the video end?

Ⓐ 9:50 A.M.
Ⓑ 10:30 A.M.
Ⓒ 10:40 A.M.
Ⓓ 10:50 A.M.
Ⓔ NG

GO ON ⟹

Practice Test 3 *(continued)*

16. If you spin the spinner 20 times, which number will the spinner probably land on most often?

Ⓕ 2
Ⓖ 3
Ⓗ 4
Ⓙ 5
Ⓚ NG

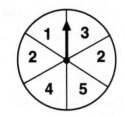

17. At Joe's Adventure Golf, golf balls are kept in a large box. The chart shows how many balls of each color are in the box.

Color	Number
Red	24
Blue	12
Yellow	68
Green	20
Purple	35

If you reach into the box without looking and take one golf ball, which color are you most likely to get?

Ⓐ red
Ⓑ blue
Ⓒ yellow
Ⓓ green
Ⓔ NG

18. Keith uses 5 lemons to make 2 pitchers of lemonade.

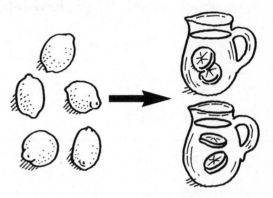

At this rate, how many lemons would Keith use to make 12 pitchers of lemonade?

Ⓕ 12
Ⓖ 15
Ⓗ 20
Ⓙ 30
Ⓚ NG

19. Five children were sitting in a row on a bench. Bob sat on one end. Lee sat between Bob and Jim. Pete sat next to Jim. Peg sat next to Pete. If Bob was sitting at one end of the bench, who was sitting at the other end?

Ⓐ Peg
Ⓑ Lee
Ⓒ Pete
Ⓓ Jim
Ⓔ NG

GO ON ⇨

Practice Test 3 *(continued)*

20. Carla had $100. She spent $32.00 on groceries and $26.00 for gasoline. How much money did she have left?

- Ⓕ $42.00
- Ⓖ $58.00
- Ⓗ $68.00
- Ⓙ $74.00
- Ⓚ NG

21. Mr. Harrison drove 1150 miles in March, 2180 miles in April, and 1937 miles in May. <u>About</u> how many miles in all did he drive in these 3 months?

- Ⓐ 3,000
- Ⓑ 4,000
- Ⓒ 5,000
- Ⓓ 6,000

22. Sam bought 50 stamps for $0.34 each. <u>About</u> how much did he spend on stamps?

- Ⓕ $1.50–$2.00
- Ⓖ $5.00–$8.00
- Ⓗ $15.00–$20.00
- Ⓙ $150.00–$200.00

23. Members of the Kids' Club held a car wash one day to make money. They washed 74 cars in all. What else do you need to know to figure out how much money they made?

- Ⓐ how much they charged for each car
- Ⓑ what day the car wash was held
- Ⓒ how many members are in the club
- Ⓓ where the car wash was held
- Ⓔ NG

24. Sharon saved $620 last year. Her sister Kayla saved $75.00 less than that. How much did Kayla save?

- Ⓕ $535
- Ⓖ $545
- Ⓗ $555
- Ⓙ $695
- Ⓚ NG

25. Grace is reading a book that is 260 pages long. She read 24 pages on Monday, 30 pages on Tuesday, and 25 pages on Wednesday. How many pages does she have left to read?

- Ⓐ 79
- Ⓑ 181
- Ⓒ 206
- Ⓓ 230
- Ⓔ NG

STOP

Practice Test 4
Reading

Directions. Choose the word that means the same as the underlined word. Mark your answer.

1. <u>under</u> the table
- Ⓐ beneath
- Ⓑ around
- Ⓒ above
- Ⓓ beside

2. a famous <u>author</u>
- Ⓕ leader
- Ⓖ actor
- Ⓗ musician
- Ⓙ writer

3. heard him <u>bragging</u>
- Ⓐ crying
- Ⓑ boasting
- Ⓒ working
- Ⓓ singing

4. an act of <u>courage</u>
- Ⓕ kindness
- Ⓖ bravery
- Ⓗ wisdom
- Ⓙ weakness

5. everything you could <u>desire</u>
- Ⓐ deserve
- Ⓑ remember
- Ⓒ want
- Ⓓ take

Directions. Choose the word that means the **oppposite** of the underlined word. Mark your answer.

6. about to <u>depart</u>
- Ⓕ open
- Ⓖ arrive
- Ⓗ finish
- Ⓙ rise

7. a <u>fancy</u> dress
- Ⓐ simple
- Ⓑ long
- Ⓒ colorful
- Ⓓ clean

8. in the <u>future</u>
- Ⓕ time
- Ⓖ direction
- Ⓗ place
- Ⓙ past

9. a <u>humble</u> person
- Ⓐ smart
- Ⓑ happy
- Ⓒ proud
- Ⓓ lazy

10. to <u>borrow</u> a few dollars
- Ⓕ find
- Ⓖ lend
- Ⓗ earn
- Ⓙ spend

GO ON ➡

Practice Test 4 *(continued)*

Directions. Read each passage. Choose the best answer to each question. Mark your answer.

Double Divers

Emily Bouck and Chelsea Davis have their eyes on the prize. They put in long hours at a swimming pool practicing difficult dives. If their hard work pays off, Emily and Chelsea will represent the United States at the 2004 Olympics in an exciting new sport.

You might think that diving has been an Olympic sport for ages, but Emily and Chelsea do synchronized diving, a sport you've probably never seen. In synchronized diving, two divers perform together on side-by-side diving boards. They try to time their movements so that they spring from the board, do their mid-air spins, and knife into the water at exactly the same time.

Synchronized diving is very difficult. It's hard enough for one diver to perform a beautiful dive, but it's twice as hard for two divers to do the same beautiful dive together. Emily and Chelsea think they have what it takes to succeed, though. To find out if they're right, watch the 2004 Summer Olympics.

11. What is this story mostly about?
- (A) a swimming pool
- (B) the Summer Olympics
- (C) two best friends
- (D) a new Olympic diving sport

12. Which sentence best describes synchronized diving?
- (F) Emily Bouck and Chelsea Davis have their eyes on the prize.
- (G) Two divers perform together on side-by-side diving boards.
- (H) It's hard enough for one diver to perform a beautiful dive.
- (J) Watch the 2004 Summer Olympics.

13. Which information shows that Emily and Chelsea work hard at their sport?
- (A) They put in long hours at the pool.
- (B) They have their eye on the prize.
- (C) They try to time their movements.
- (D) They may compete at the 2004 Olympics.

14. As they get ready for the 2004 Summer Olympics, Emily and Chelsea probably feel —
- (F) bored
- (G) afraid
- (H) determined
- (J) disappointed

GO ON

Practice Test 4 *(continued)*

Win a Trip to Washington, D.C.

Washington, D.C., is our nation's capital and home to the President of the United States. It's also a great place to visit! Enter *Rightstuff* magazine's "Why I'll Make a Great President" Contest for a chance to win a trip to this important city.

FIRST PRIZE: A two-day trip to Washington, D.C., for the winner and one adult companion. Prize includes airplane tickets, two nights in a hotel, meals, and tours of the White House, the Lincoln Memorial, and the Washington Monument.
HONOR PRIZES: A White House T-shirt and cap.

To enter:
1. Write an essay that tells why you will make a great President. Your essay should be 100–200 words and must be typed or neatly printed.
2. On the back of your essay, write your name, date of birth, and address. (You must be between the ages of 9 and 12 by May 31.)
3. Mail your essay by May 31. Send it to *Rightstuff* Great President Contest, P.O. Box 25, Columbus, OH 43216.
4. One first-prize winner and ten honor-prize winners will be chosen. All winners will be notified by mail, and their names will appear in *Rightstuff*.

---

15. This announcement was written to —
- Ⓐ give information about a contest
- Ⓑ tell how to become President
- Ⓒ describe *Rightstuff* magazine
- Ⓓ list places in Washington, D.C.

16. Which sentence about Washington, D.C., is an opinion?
- Ⓕ It is our nation's capital.
- Ⓖ The White House is there.
- Ⓗ It is a great place to visit.
- Ⓙ The President lives there.

17. You can enter the contest if you are —
- Ⓐ 8 years old
- Ⓑ 10 years old
- Ⓒ 13 years old
- Ⓓ 15 years old

18. Who could take the trip with the first-prize winner?
- Ⓕ one parent
- Ⓖ two parents and one child
- Ⓗ two grandparents
- Ⓙ a brother or a sister

19. Each honor-prize winner will receive —
- Ⓐ *Rightstuff* magazine
- Ⓑ airplane tickets
- Ⓒ a tour of the White House
- Ⓓ a T-shirt and cap

Practice Test 4 *(continued)*

To the Editor:

Last week I solved a problem many of your readers probably have. The problem is serious, but the solution is easy. Do what I did, and you'll help the environment.

I discovered the problem while taking out the trash. We usually have two bags, but last week there was an extra bag, and it was really heavy. I opened it and saw about 40 catalogs! What's up with this, I wondered, so I asked my mother. She said that every month we get catalogs in the mail from companies that want us to order their products. She throws them out, but each company sends a new catalog the next month.

I took the catalogs out of the bag and asked my mother to show me the ones she actually uses. There were only three! I looked at the others and thought about the trees they were made from and the landfill space they would take up when we got rid of them. I wanted to find a way to stop the waste.

I did. Inside each catalog I found a toll-free telephone number. I stacked up the catalogs my mother never uses and started dialing. I asked each telephone representative to take our family off the mailing list. Each one politely agreed and thanked me for calling. Problem solved!

Kenny Blasedale
Hullsville

 GO ON

Practice Test 4 (continued)

20. Kenny's main reason for writing this letter is to —
- Ⓕ tell a story about himself
- Ⓖ convince others to cut down on the number of catalogs they get
- Ⓗ explain how to order products through the mail
- Ⓙ tell which catalogs his family uses

21. Kenny sent this letter to —
- Ⓐ the landfill in his town
- Ⓑ his classmates
- Ⓒ telephone representatives
- Ⓓ the newspaper

22. Which sentence states an opinion?
- Ⓕ The problem is serious, but the solution is easy.
- Ⓖ I discovered the problem while taking out the trash.
- Ⓗ Every month we get catalogs in the mail.
- Ⓙ Each company sends a new catalog the next month.

23. Which information best shows how much waste the bag of catalogs made?
- Ⓐ Kenny discovered the problem while taking out the trash.
- Ⓑ The catalogs come in the mail.
- Ⓒ Kenny's mother used only three out of the 40 catalogs she got.
- Ⓓ Each catalog lists a toll-free number.

24. Kenny called the telephone representatives to —
- Ⓕ find out more about each company
- Ⓖ see what products they sold
- Ⓗ ask for the newest catalogs
- Ⓙ have his family taken off their mailing lists

25. You can tell that Kenny is a boy who cares about —
- Ⓐ protecting the environment
- Ⓑ finding ways to make his chores easier
- Ⓒ buying new things for himself
- Ⓓ proving how grown-up he is

Practice Test 4
Mathematics

Directions. Choose the best answer to each question. Mark your answer. If the correct answer is *not given,* choose "NG."

1.
$$\begin{array}{r} 317 \\ 84 \\ +\ 129 \\ \hline \end{array}$$

  Ⓐ 420
  Ⓑ 430
  Ⓒ 510
  Ⓓ 530
  Ⓔ NG

2.
$$\begin{array}{r} 602 \\ -\ 51 \\ \hline \end{array}$$

  Ⓕ 653
  Ⓖ 651
  Ⓗ 553
  Ⓙ 541
  Ⓚ NG

3.
$$\begin{array}{r} 487 \\ -\ 219 \\ \hline \end{array}$$

  Ⓐ 252
  Ⓑ 262
  Ⓒ 268
  Ⓓ 278
  Ⓔ NG

4. This chart shows the number of pies sold each day at a bakery.

Pies Sold	
Tuesday	8
Wednesday	12
Thursday	20
Friday	24

What was the average number of pies sold each day?
  Ⓕ 12
  Ⓖ 16
  Ⓗ 24
  Ⓙ 64
  Ⓚ NG

5. Mr. James took 3 flights this week.

Flight	Distance (miles)
Seattle–Salem	212
Salem–Boise	433
Boise–Seattle	487

How many miles did he fly in all?
  Ⓐ 1122
  Ⓑ 1132
  Ⓒ 1222
  Ⓓ 1232
  Ⓔ NG

GO ON ▷

Practice Test 4 *(continued)*

6.   75
        × 4

Ⓕ 260
Ⓖ 275
Ⓗ 280
Ⓙ 300
Ⓚ NG

7.   519
        × 3

Ⓐ 1554
Ⓑ 1547
Ⓒ 1537
Ⓓ 1534
Ⓔ NG

8.   60
        × 20

Ⓕ 120
Ⓖ 800
Ⓗ 1200
Ⓙ 1220
Ⓚ NG

9. 8 × □ = 56

Ⓐ 5
Ⓑ 6
Ⓒ 7
Ⓓ 8
Ⓔ NG

10. Paul has 4 different colored T-shirts and 2 pairs of shorts.

4   2

How many different combinations of one T-shirt and a pair of shorts can he wear?

Ⓕ 12
Ⓖ 8
Ⓗ 6
Ⓙ 4
Ⓚ NG

11. Lena has these hair ties in a drawer.

Color	Number
Red	4
Yellow	5
Black	8
White	3

If Lena takes one hair tie out of the drawer without looking, what is the probability that she will choose a yellow one?

Ⓐ $\frac{1}{4}$

Ⓑ $\frac{5}{10}$

Ⓒ $\frac{1}{20}$

Ⓓ $\frac{1}{5}$

Ⓔ NG

GO ON ⇨

Practice Test 4 *(continued)*

12. $32 \div 4 =$

  Ⓕ 4
  Ⓖ 6
  Ⓗ 7
  Ⓙ 9
  Ⓚ NG

13. $7\overline{)63}$

  Ⓐ 7
  Ⓑ 8
  Ⓒ 9
  Ⓓ 11
  Ⓔ NG

14. $4\overline{)84}$

  Ⓕ 20
  Ⓖ 21
  Ⓗ 22
  Ⓙ 31
  Ⓚ NG

15. $3\overline{)960}$

  Ⓐ 32
  Ⓑ 310
  Ⓒ 318
  Ⓓ 320
  Ⓔ NG

16. The grid shows where five points are located.

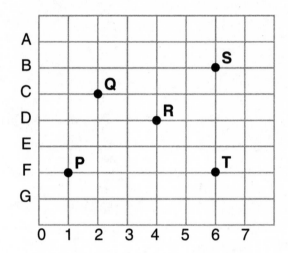

Which point is located at 6B?

  Ⓕ point P
  Ⓖ point Q
  Ⓗ point R
  Ⓙ point S
  Ⓚ NG

17. Ms. Teplick wrote this number sentence on the blackboard.

$(16 + n) - 5 = 30$

What is the value of *n?*

  Ⓐ 19
  Ⓑ 20
  Ⓒ 29
  Ⓓ 35
  Ⓔ NG

GO ON

Practice Test 4 (continued)

18. This chart shows the number of books students read in the summer reading program.

Books Read	
Megan	15
Carl	6
Trudy	9
Ronnie	10

What was the average number of books read per student?

Ⓕ 40
Ⓖ 15
Ⓗ 10
Ⓙ 9
Ⓚ NG

19. Harry wrote this number sentence to solve a problem.

$(8 \times n) - 4 = 20$

What is the value of *n*?

Ⓐ 2
Ⓑ 4
Ⓒ 6
Ⓓ 8
Ⓔ NG

The grid below shows the location of six shapes. Use the grid to answer questions 20 and 21.

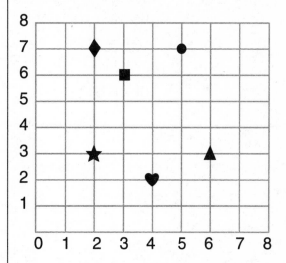

20. What shape is located at (6, 3)?

Ⓕ ♥
Ⓖ ▲
Ⓗ ★
Ⓙ ■
Ⓚ NG

21. What is the location of the ◆ ?

Ⓐ (7, 2)
Ⓑ (3, 6)
Ⓒ (2, 3)
Ⓓ (2, 7)
Ⓔ NG

GO ON

Practice Test 4 (continued)

22. $\frac{3}{5} + \frac{1}{5} =$

   (F) $\frac{3}{5}$

   (G) $\frac{3}{25}$

   (H) $\frac{4}{5}$

   (J) $\frac{4}{10}$

   (K) NG

23.

$$\begin{array}{r} \frac{1}{8} \\ + \frac{5}{8} \\ \hline \end{array}$$

   (A) $\frac{3}{4}$

   (B) $\frac{4}{8}$

   (C) $\frac{6}{16}$

   (D) $\frac{3}{8}$

   (E) NG

24.

$$\begin{array}{r} \frac{9}{10} \\ - \frac{3}{10} \\ \hline \end{array}$$

   (F) $1\frac{2}{10}$

   (G) $\frac{3}{5}$

   (H) $\frac{6}{20}$

   (J) $\frac{5}{10}$

   (K) NG

25. $4.5 + 7.1 =$

   (A) 12.6

   (B) 11.6

   (C) 10.6

   (D) 2.6

   (E) NG

26. $13.28 + 9.7 =$

   (F) 21.98

   (G) 22.35

   (H) 22.88

   (J) 23.08

   (K) NG

27.

$$\begin{array}{r} \$36.50 \\ - 28.99 \\ \hline \end{array}$$

   (A) $8.59

   (B) $8.49

   (C) $7.91

   (D) $7.51

   (E) NG

28. $24.05 - 16.8 =$

   (F) 8.30

   (G) 8.03

   (H) 7.70

   (J) 7.25

   (K) NG

STOP

Practice Test 5
Reading
Directions. Choose the meaning of the underlined word. Mark your answer.

1. To <u>divide</u> means to —
- Ⓐ begin
- Ⓑ separate
- Ⓒ accept
- Ⓓ improve

2. Something that is <u>accurate</u> is —
- Ⓕ correct
- Ⓖ new
- Ⓗ large
- Ⓙ peaceful

3. A <u>conversation</u> is a —
- Ⓐ drawing
- Ⓑ house
- Ⓒ talk
- Ⓓ tool

4. To <u>doze</u> means to —
- Ⓕ push
- Ⓖ help
- Ⓗ watch
- Ⓙ nap

5. A <u>pastry</u> is a kind of —
- Ⓐ report
- Ⓑ glue
- Ⓒ food
- Ⓓ cloth

6. <u>Fearsome</u> means —
- Ⓕ sudden
- Ⓖ frightening
- Ⓗ special
- Ⓙ timid

7. A <u>jersey</u> is a kind of —
- Ⓐ shirt
- Ⓑ rope
- Ⓒ vehicle
- Ⓓ plant

8. To <u>link</u> means to —
- Ⓕ start over
- Ⓖ raise
- Ⓗ join together
- Ⓙ answer

9. A <u>nudge</u> is —
- Ⓐ a whisper
- Ⓑ a thought
- Ⓒ an ache
- Ⓓ a push

10. <u>Bewildered</u> means —
- Ⓕ confused
- Ⓖ loud
- Ⓗ serious
- Ⓙ careful

11. To <u>educate</u> means to —
- Ⓐ enjoy
- Ⓑ teach
- Ⓒ build
- Ⓓ replace

12. Something that is <u>coarse</u> is —
- Ⓕ neat
- Ⓖ quick
- Ⓗ tiny
- Ⓙ rough

GO ON ⇨

Practice Test 5 *(continued*

Directions. Read each passage. Choose the best answer to each question. Mark your answer.

The Race

One day a hungry fox saw a crab inching across the sand. "What a tasty snack I shall have!" said the fox. Then he snapped up the crab in his mouth.

The crab was a slow creature, but he had a good head on his shoulders. "Let's have a race," he suggested. "If you win, you may eat me. If I win, you must set me free."

The fox was sure he had nothing to lose. He accepted the crab's challenge, saying, "We'll count to three and go." Then the crab and the fox began counting, "One, two —" Just on the count of three, the crab jumped up and hid himself in the fox's bushy tail. The fox took off running, while the crab held on tight and enjoyed the speedy ride. As he ran, the fox kept glancing backward, but he could not see the crab. At last the fox slowed to a stop. Then he turned around and said, "I've left that crab far behind, and now I will go back and eat him."

At that instant, the crab let go of the fox's tail and dropped to the ground. "Turn around, Fox," said the crab, "and see for yourself that I am the winner of the race!"

The fox was too surprised to speak, so he simply walked away to find something else to eat. Try as he might, he never did figure out how the crab finished the race ahead of him.

13. The story says that the crab "had a good head on his shoulders." This means that the crab —
- (A) stood on his head
- (B) was clever
- (C) could look in every direction
- (D) was very handsome

14. How did the fox feel as he got ready to race the crab?
- (F) frustrated
- (G) puzzled
- (H) confident
- (J) foolish

15. The fox couldn't see the crab when he glanced backward because the crab was —
- (A) back at the starting line
- (B) stuck in the sand
- (C) way ahead of the fox
- (D) hiding in the fox's tail

16. What lesson does this story teach?
- (F) Think your way out of trouble.
- (G) Let others win sometimes.
- (H) Be kind to small creatures.
- (J) Never accept a challenge.

Practice Test 5 *(continued)*

Letter from a Pioneer Teacher

September 9, 1869

Dear Mother and Father,

    I've just finished my first week of teaching here in Thurston, and I can see that the job will be challenging. I teach in a one-room school built by the children's parents. Like all the homes here, the school is made of sod bricks cut from the ground and dried in the sun. (No one here builds with lumber, which must be brought hundreds of miles by train and is very expensive.) The children sit on benches, but I am lucky to have a desk. Until a well can be dug for the school, the children will take turns bringing water from their own wells by wagon.

    Last week I had only ten children, ages 7 to 13, but their older brothers and sisters will join us after the fall harvest. Most of the children are ready to learn, but a few are mainly interested in making mischief. I can't really blame them, though. These children rise at dawn to milk cows and feed chickens, and some walk three or four miles to school. Still, I plan to run a tight ship so that they may learn all I have to teach them.

Your loving daughter,
Rebecca

17. How is the school like the homes in Thurston?
- Ⓐ It has a well.
- Ⓑ It is made of sod.
- Ⓒ It has benches and desks.
- Ⓓ It has several rooms.

18. What does this letter suggest about Thurston?
- Ⓕ It is a large city.
- Ⓖ It has terrible weather.
- Ⓗ It has hardly any trees.
- Ⓙ It has many streams and ponds.

19. The children rise at dawn to —
- Ⓐ milk cows and gather eggs
- Ⓑ play with their friends
- Ⓒ make mischief
- Ⓓ do their school lessons

20. Older children did not go to school the first week because —
- Ⓕ there was not enough room for them
- Ⓖ they were helping with the fall harvest
- Ⓗ they did not know about the school yet
- Ⓙ they did not like their new teacher

21. Rebecca plans to "run a tight ship." This means that she will —
- Ⓐ make the children work hard
- Ⓑ teach the children about oceans
- Ⓒ take a trip on a ship
- Ⓓ keep the school warm and cozy

GO ON

After Goldie

Dr. Marco gave Dave the bad news. "You're allergic to feathers, and that's why you've been having trouble breathing."

"Can't you give me medicine to make me better?" asked Dave.

Dr. Marco shook her head no, and Mom said, "You'll have to give away Goldie."

At his next check-up, Dave's breathing trouble was gone. Mom and Dr. Marco were pleased—but not Dave. He had hoped they were mistaken about Goldie so that he could get her back. Dave felt empty inside on the way home. Mom brought up the idea of a different pet for Dave. "How about tropical fish," she asked, "or maybe a lizard or a snake?"

"No way!" Dave answered. "Goldie sings and chirps. She flutters around and dangles upside down from her perch. That's the kind of pet I want."

A few days later, a package came in the mail for Dave. Inside the package was a birdfeeder. It was a plastic tube with perches attached to it.

"I ordered the feeder because I know how much you miss Goldie," said Mom. Then she took a bag of birdseed from the kitchen cupboard. "Let's fill up the birdfeeder and hang it outside your bedroom window."

For the next few days, Dave checked the birdfeeder often, but he always found it empty. Then one morning, he woke up to the sound of chirping. Dave jumped out of bed and ran to the window. He thought he might see a red cardinal or maybe a brown sparrow, but what he saw made him gasp with delight. "Come see this, Mom!" he exclaimed.

Mom ran and looked out the window. Then she said, "Your first customer is a goldfinch. He looks a bit like Goldie, doesn't he?"

Dave laughed. "He looks *just* like Goldie except for the black cap!"

The goldfinch fluttered its wings and hopped to the highest perch. It dangled upside down for a moment, pecking at some birdseed. Then it flew off to a nearby tree.

Dave sighed and said, "That was a short visit. I hope he'll come back."

"He'll be back all right," Mom replied. "Just listen to his chirping—he's inviting his friends and family to breakfast at Dave's house!"

Practice Test 5 *(continued)*

22. Why did Dave have to give away Goldie?
- Ⓕ Goldie's feathers made him sick.
- Ⓖ He wanted a different kind of pet.
- Ⓗ Mom didn't like Goldie.
- Ⓙ He didn't take good care of Goldie.

23. The story says that Dave "felt empty inside on the way home." This means that Dave —
- Ⓐ hadn't eaten for a while
- Ⓑ was getting sick
- Ⓒ felt sad and lonely
- Ⓓ was afraid of something

24. How did Dave feel when his breathing problem went away?
- Ⓕ happy
- Ⓖ disappointed
- Ⓗ amazed
- Ⓙ relieved

25. When Dave had to give away Goldie, Dave's mom tried to make him feel better by —
- Ⓐ taking him to a new doctor
- Ⓑ ordering a new pet bird for him
- Ⓒ giving him a ride home
- Ⓓ suggesting a different kind of pet

26. What color do you think Goldie was?
- Ⓕ red
- Ⓖ brown
- Ⓗ blue
- Ⓙ yellow

27. How was the goldfinch at the birdfeeder different from Goldie?
- Ⓐ He had a black head.
- Ⓑ He lived in a cage.
- Ⓒ He ate birdseed.
- Ⓓ He dangled upside down.

28. What kind of story is this?
- Ⓕ historical fiction
- Ⓖ a fairy tale
- Ⓗ realistic fiction
- Ⓙ a myth

Practice Test 5
Mathematics
Directions. Choose the best answer to each question. Mark your answer.

1. The highest mountain in Kansas is 4039 feet. Which words mean 4039?

Ⓐ forty thousand thirty-nine

Ⓑ four thousand thirty-nine

Ⓒ four thousand three hundred nine

Ⓓ four hundred thirty-nine

2. What goes in the box to make this number sentence true?

$7 \times 3 = \square$

Ⓕ 3×7

Ⓖ $7 + 3$

Ⓗ $7 \div 3$

Ⓙ $7 - 3$

3. Which basketball player made the most free throws?

Name	Free Throws Made
Mark Price	2135
Rick Barry	3818
Calvin Murphy	3445
Scott Skiles	1548
Larry Bird	3960

Ⓐ Mark Price

Ⓑ Rick Barry

Ⓒ Calvin Murphy

Ⓓ Larry Bird

4. What fractional part of this figure is shaded?

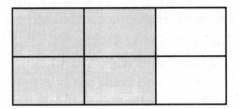

Ⓕ $\dfrac{5}{6}$ Ⓗ $\dfrac{2}{3}$

Ⓖ $\dfrac{1}{2}$ Ⓙ $\dfrac{2}{4}$

5. Which number is equal to $(3 \times 1000) + (8 \times 100) + (9 \times 1)$?

Ⓐ 389   Ⓒ 3809

Ⓑ 3089   Ⓓ 3890

6. The chart shows how much maple syrup Chad made one week.

Day	Maple Syrup Made
Sunday	$\frac{1}{2}$ gallon
Tuesday	$\frac{3}{4}$ gallon
Thursday	$\frac{5}{8}$ gallon
Saturday	$\frac{1}{3}$ gallon

On which day did Chad make the most syrup?

Ⓕ Sunday   Ⓗ Thursday

Ⓖ Tuesday   Ⓙ Saturday

GO ON

Practice Test 5 *(continued)*

7. Which address is an even number?
- Ⓐ 84 Lemon Road
- Ⓑ 75 Elm Street
- Ⓒ 99 Fifth Street
- Ⓓ 61 Morgan Road

8. Which figure shows $\frac{3}{5}$ shaded?

Ⓕ   Ⓗ

Ⓖ   Ⓙ

9. This table shows the number of points Josh scored in each basketball game.

Game	1	2	3	4	5	6
Points	7	12	17	22	27	

If this pattern continues, what number should go in the box for Game 6?
- Ⓐ 29
- Ⓑ 30
- Ⓒ 32
- Ⓓ 37

This chart lists the length of the shoreline in each of six states. Use the chart to answer questions 10 and 11.

Shoreline of U.S. States	
State	**Shoreline (miles)**
Georgia	2344
Maine	3478
Maryland	3190
Massachusetts	1519
New Jersey	1792
Virginia	2876

10. Which of these states has the longest shoreline?
- Ⓕ Georgia
- Ⓖ Maine
- Ⓗ Maryland
- Ⓙ Virginia

11. Which state has a longer shoreline than Massachusetts but shorter than Georgia?
- Ⓐ Maryland
- Ⓑ Maine
- Ⓒ Virginia
- Ⓓ New Jersey

GO ON ⇨

Practice Test 5 *(continued)*

12. Ms. Falco paid $8675 for rent last year. What is that amount rounded to the nearest hundred dollars?

Ⓕ $8000
Ⓖ $8600
Ⓗ $8700
Ⓙ $9000

13. Stella drove 607 miles last week. What is that number rounded to the nearest ten?

Ⓐ 700
Ⓑ 650
Ⓒ 610
Ⓓ 600

14. What goes in the box to make the number sentence true?

$(16 + 4) + 5 = (4 + 5) + \square$

Ⓕ 7
Ⓖ 10
Ⓗ 12
Ⓙ 16

15. A new book costs $19.95. <u>About</u> how much would 50 of these books cost?

Ⓐ $70–$80
Ⓑ $90–$100
Ⓒ $700–$800
Ⓓ $900–$1000

16. Which number sentence is correct?

Ⓕ $1 \times 5 = 15$
Ⓖ $5 \times 0 = 0$
Ⓗ $5 \times 1 = 5 + 1$
Ⓙ $0 \times 5 = 5 \times 1$

17. Hal made this pattern of shapes

If the pattern continues, what shape should come next?

Ⓐ □

Ⓑ ⇨

Ⓒ ◇

Ⓓ ⇦

GO ON

Practice Test 5 *(continued)*

18. Which pair of numbers are factors of 56?

   Ⓕ 7, 8

   Ⓖ 4, 12

   Ⓗ 9, 6

   Ⓙ 5, 11

19. The Allegheny Tunnel in Pennsylvania is six thousand seventy-two feet long. Which number means six thousand seventy-two?

   Ⓐ 672

   Ⓑ 6072

   Ⓒ 6720

   Ⓓ 60,072

20. Which ZIP code is an odd number?

   Ⓕ 97420

   Ⓖ 22308

   Ⓗ 15501

   Ⓙ 78336

21. What number is equal to $(4 \times 1000) + (9 \times 100) + (7 \times 10)$?

   Ⓐ 40,970

   Ⓑ 4907

   Ⓒ 4097

   Ⓓ 4970

22. Which number has a 5 in the thousands place?

   Ⓕ 2415

   Ⓖ 3580

   Ⓗ 5721

   Ⓙ 8350

23. A total of 6120 people went to the zoo on Saturday to see the pandas, and 8870 went on Sunday. Which numbers would give the best estimate of the total number of people who went to the zoo for both days?

   Ⓐ 6000 + 8000

   Ⓑ 7000 + 8000

   Ⓒ 6000 + 9000

   Ⓓ 7000 + 9000

GO ON ⟹

Practice Test 5 *(continued)*

24. Which fact is in the same family as $9 - 4 = 5$?

  Ⓕ $5 + 4 = 9$
  Ⓖ $9 + 5 = 14$
  Ⓗ $9 + 4 = 13$
  Ⓙ $5 - 4 = 1$

25. The numbers 3, 6, and 9 are all factors of what number?

  Ⓐ 18
  Ⓑ 24
  Ⓒ 27
  Ⓓ 30

26. Which figure shows thirty-six hundredths shaded?

Ⓕ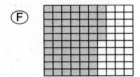

Ⓖ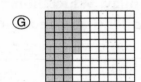

Ⓗ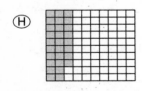

Ⓙ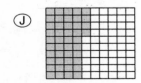

27. Mr. James wanted to buy a barrel. He compared how many gallons of water each barrel could hold.

Barrel	Capacity (gal)
1	$18\frac{3}{4}$
2	$17\frac{9}{10}$
3	$18\frac{1}{3}$
4	$17\frac{7}{8}$

Which barrel holds the most?

  Ⓐ Barrel 1
  Ⓑ Barrel 2
  Ⓒ Barrel 3
  Ⓓ Barrel 4

28. Four people won a prize of $10,500. Each person will get an equal share of the prize. Which number sentence should be used to find the amount that each person should get?

  Ⓕ $\$10,500 \times 4 = \square$
  Ⓖ $\$10,500 + 4 = \square$
  Ⓗ $\$10,500 - 4 = \square$
  Ⓙ $\$10,500 \div 4 = \square$

STOP

Practice Test 6

Reading

Directions. Read the sentence in the box. Choose the answer in which the underlined word has the same meaning. Mark your answer.

1. | Rest your <u>head</u> on the pillow. |

In which sentence does <u>head</u> have the same meaning?
- Ⓐ Stand at the <u>head</u> of the line.
- Ⓑ Please pick out a <u>head</u> of lettuce.
- Ⓒ We should <u>head</u> home now.
- Ⓓ Turn your <u>head</u> to the left.

2. | You should write a thank-you <u>note</u>. |

In which sentence does <u>note</u> have the same meaning?
- Ⓕ Can Wanda sing the high <u>note</u>?
- Ⓖ <u>Note</u> how tall this tree grew.
- Ⓗ Leave a <u>note</u> for your parents.
- Ⓙ Let's end our trip on a good <u>note</u>.

3. | I can help you <u>tie</u> that ribbon. |

In which sentence does <u>tie</u> have the same meaning?
- Ⓐ <u>Tie</u> this sash around your waist.
- Ⓑ The horse race ended in a <u>tie</u>.
- Ⓒ The accident may <u>tie</u> up traffic.
- Ⓓ Ollie wore a coat and <u>tie</u>.

4. | I think the phone will <u>work</u> now. |

In which sentence does <u>work</u> have the same meaning?
- Ⓕ Hank has drawn a <u>work</u> of art.
- Ⓖ Alice's <u>work</u> is almost done.
- Ⓗ Can you get this clock to <u>work</u>?
- Ⓙ Our coaches <u>work</u> us too hard!

5. | Let's read from the <u>top</u> of the page. |

In which sentence does <u>top</u> have the same meaning?
- Ⓐ No one can <u>top</u> that story!
- Ⓑ We'll walk to the <u>top</u> of the hill.
- Ⓒ Put the <u>top</u> on the toothpaste.
- Ⓓ The girls ran at <u>top</u> speed.

6. | This old pot is made of <u>iron</u>. |

In which sentence does <u>iron</u> have the same meaning?
- Ⓕ Be sure to <u>iron</u> those pants.
- Ⓖ These <u>iron</u> tools rust easily.
- Ⓗ Don't touch that hot <u>iron</u>!
- Ⓙ We can <u>iron</u> out our problems.

GO ON ▷

Practice Test 6 *(continued)*
Directions. Read each passage. Choose the best answer to each question. Mark your answer.

SUMMER ART CLASSES

Everybody loves art. This year, the Arts Center is offering summer art classes for kids who want to learn new skills and have lots of fun, too. Call 555-1432 to sign up. Classes fill up quickly, so don't delay!

Class 1: Clay for Beginners
Ages: 8–12 Teacher: Sally Merriam
Mondays and Wednesdays, 9–10 A.M.
Learn how to shape and mold clay with your hands and simple tools. Make masks, sculptures, and containers.

Class 3: Oil Painting
Ages: 8 and up Teacher: Bernie Kofax
Tuesdays and Thursdays, 10–11 A.M.
Learn to prepare a canvas, and mix and apply oil paints. Paint a self-portrait from a photograph of yourself.

Class 2: Painting with Watercolors
Ages: 8 and up Teacher: Bernie Kofax
Tuesdays and Thursdays, 9–10 A.M.
Learn to create soft or bold effects with watercolors. Paint people, animals, outdoor scenes, and more!

Class 4: Using a Potter's Wheel
Ages: 12 and up Teacher: Sally Merriam
Mondays and Wednesdays, 10–11 A.M.
Learn to make pots, vases, and bowls on a potter's wheel. Please note: This class is not for beginners!

---

7. The notice says, "Don't delay!" What does delay mean?
- Ⓐ call
- Ⓑ watch
- Ⓒ wait
- Ⓓ try

8. Which sentence is a generalization?
- Ⓕ The Arts Center has summer classes.
- Ⓖ Everybody loves art.
- Ⓗ You can make masks in Class 1.
- Ⓙ Class 3 is an oil painting class.

9. Which class is probably the hardest?
- Ⓐ Clay for Beginners
- Ⓑ Painting with Watercolors
- Ⓒ Oil Painting
- Ⓓ Using a Potter's Wheel

10. What can you tell about Bernie Kofax from this notice?
- Ⓕ He likes to make pottery.
- Ⓖ He knows how to paint.
- Ⓗ He is a high school teacher.
- Ⓙ He owns many cameras.

GO ON ▷

Practice Test 6 *(continued)*

Family Matters

Eleven-year-old Aimee Lamb, her brother Eric, and their parents had to make a big decision back in 1999. An adoption agency had sent them photographs of children in China who needed homes. The Lambs were looking through the photos, trying to decide which child might become a new member of their family.

The Lambs were drawn to the picture of an 11-year-old girl named Xiao Fang (pronounced show-FONG). They just knew she was meant to be part of their family, so Mr. and Mrs. Lamb filled out the adoption papers. Then the waiting began. The Lambs knew it would take months to <u>finalize</u> the adoption.

On the other side of the world, Xiao Fang was also waiting. She tried to imagine what an American family might be like. To help Xiao Fang, Aimee sent her an album filled with photos of the Lambs and their home.

Finally, word came from the adoption agency that the Lambs could bring Xiao Fang to the United States. Aimee and her mother flew to China, and an adoption worker brought Xiao Fang to their hotel to meet them. Xiao Fang walked into the hotel room clutching the album from Aimee. She smiled at her new mother and sister and talked excitedly in Chinese. Then Mrs. Lamb asked if she should call Xiao Fang by her Chinese name or by her new American name, Emily. When the worker repeated the question to Xiao Fang in Chinese, she exclaimed, "Emily!"

11. **What is this article mainly about?**
(A) where the Lambs live
(B) how the Lambs adopted Xiao Fang
(C) what life is like in China
(D) why Xiao Fang changed her name

12. **It took months to <u>finalize</u> the adoption. What does <u>finalize</u> mean?**
(F) repeat   (H) complete
(G) suggest   (J) understand

13. **When Xiao Fang first met Aimee and Mrs. Lamb, she —**
(A) could not speak English
(B) took some photos of them
(C) seemed shy and nervous
(D) did not know who they were

14. **For the Lambs, what was probably the hardest thing about adopting Xiao Fang?**
(F) choosing her photo
(G) traveling to China
(H) choosing her new name
(J) waiting months to meet her

15. **The author of this article probably thinks that —**
(A) Aimee and Xiao Fang won't get along
(B) adopting a child is not worth all the trouble
(C) the Lambs and Xiao Fang are lucky to have one another
(D) every family should have three children

GO ON ⇨

Practice Test 6 *(continued)*

Making Dollars Last

Have you ever left a piece of paper in a pocket of your pants before tossing them into the wash? If you have, you know what happens next. The paper disintegrates in the washing machine and covers the laundry with wet bits of lint!

If a dollar bill goes through the wash, though, it's really not a problem. The bill gets wet and its colors may fade a bit, but it holds together. That's because a dollar bill is made from cotton and linen, just like some shirts that may be hanging in your closet.

Of course, just like a shirt, a bill won't last forever. The Bureau of Printing and Engraving in Washington, D.C., is responsible for making sure the bills we use are in good shape. The Bureau prints all the bills used in the United States. (It also prints all U.S. postage stamps.) Bills that are worn out are destroyed, and the Bureau prints fresh new bills to take their place. Old bills used to be burned, but today they are shredded, which is better for the environment.

The average one-dollar bill is shredded after just 18 months. Bills that are worth more last longer. For example, a $50-dollar bill lasts nine years. Can you guess why? Just compare how often a dollar bill and a $50 bill pass through your hands. Like most things, the more a bill gets used, the faster it wears out.

GO ON >

Practice Test 6 *(continued)*

16. This article is mostly about —
- Ⓕ dollar bills
- Ⓖ the environment
- Ⓗ laundry problems
- Ⓙ clothes

17. The article says, "The paper disintegrates in the washing machine." What does <u>disintegrates</u> mean?
- Ⓐ floats
- Ⓑ falls apart
- Ⓒ shrinks
- Ⓓ dries up

18. Bills are made from cotton and linen so that they will be —
- Ⓕ colorful
- Ⓖ stretchy
- Ⓗ soft
- Ⓙ strong

19. This article suggests that most one-dollar bills —
- Ⓐ wear out quickly
- Ⓑ will never be shredded
- Ⓒ should be washed from time to time
- Ⓓ are made from paper

20. Which detail supports the idea that government agencies try to help protect the environment?
- Ⓕ Bills are made of cotton and linen.
- Ⓖ The Bureau prints fresh new bills.
- Ⓗ Bills that are worth more last longer.
- Ⓙ Old bills are shredded, not burned.

21. The author's main purpose in writing this article was to —
- Ⓐ tell a funny story about washing money
- Ⓑ give information about the dollars we use
- Ⓒ explain how cloth is made
- Ⓓ convince people to save money

22. The author of this article seems to think that the U.S. government —
- Ⓕ wastes a lot of time and money
- Ⓖ should stop making dollar bills
- Ⓗ does a good job of printing money
- Ⓙ needs to print more $50 bills

STOP

Practice Test 6

𝔐athematics

Directions. Choose the best answer to each question. Mark your answer.

1. Which sign is a triangle?

Ⓐ

Ⓒ

Ⓑ

Ⓓ

2. Which figure has exactly 6 faces?

Ⓕ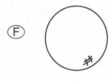

Ⓗ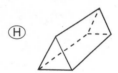

Ⓖ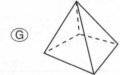

Ⓙ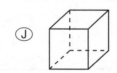

3. Which figure has only two sides that are parallel?

Ⓐ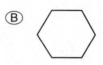

Ⓒ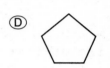

Ⓑ

Ⓓ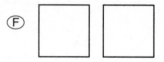

4. In which pair are the figures congruent?

Ⓕ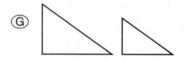

Ⓖ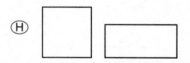

Ⓗ

Ⓙ

GO ON ⟹

Practice Test 6 *(continued)*

Use the map below to answer questions 5 and 6.

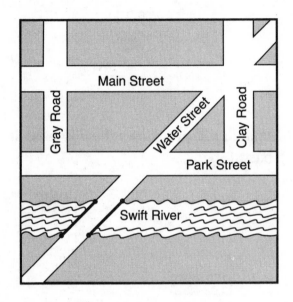

5. Which street intersects with the Swift River?
- Ⓐ Main Street
- Ⓑ Water Street
- Ⓒ Park Street
- Ⓓ Gray Road

6. Which street is parallel to Main Street?
- Ⓕ Gray Road
- Ⓖ Water Street
- Ⓗ Park Street
- Ⓙ Clay Road

The bar graph below shows the number of books sold by the Peter Pan Book Shop each week. Use the graph to answer questions 7 and 8.

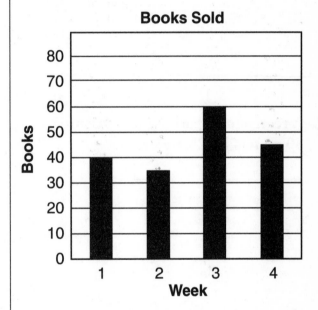

7. How many books were sold in Week 2?
- Ⓐ 45
- Ⓑ 40
- Ⓒ 35
- Ⓓ 30

8. How many more books were sold in Week 3 than in Week 4?
- Ⓕ 5
- Ⓖ 10
- Ⓗ 15
- Ⓙ 20

GO ON ⇨

Name _____ Date _____

Practice Test 6 *(continued)*

9. Which letter has a line of symmetry?

Ⓐ H   Ⓒ J

Ⓑ G   Ⓓ F

10. A rectangular parking lot measures 80 meters by 25 meters.

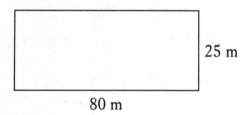

25 m

80 m

What is the perimeter of the parking lot?

Ⓕ 105 m
Ⓖ 210 m
Ⓗ 420 m
Ⓙ 2000 m

11. Which unit should be used to measure the height of a house?

Ⓐ inches
Ⓑ gallons
Ⓒ pounds
Ⓓ feet

12. This flag will be flipped to the other side of the pole when the wind changes.

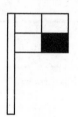

Which picture shows the flag after it has flipped?

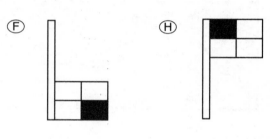

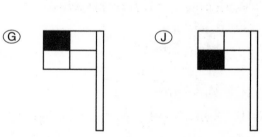

13. What time is shown on the clock?

Ⓐ 6:55
Ⓑ 10:25
Ⓒ 11:35
Ⓓ 12:35

GO ON ▷

Practice Test 6 *(continued)*

14. The floor of Lucy's rectangular bedroom is 14 feet long and 11 feet wide. What is the area of the floor?

Ⓕ 25 sq ft

Ⓖ 50 sq ft

Ⓗ 77 sq ft

Ⓙ 154 sq ft

15. A bag of 12 apples is most likely to weigh —

Ⓐ 2 ounces

Ⓑ 2 pounds

Ⓒ 2 grams

Ⓓ 2 tons

16. A truck driver drove 612 miles on Wednesday, 285 miles on Thursday, and 390 miles on Friday. <u>About</u> how far did he drive all together?

Ⓕ 900 miles

Ⓖ 1100 miles

Ⓗ 1300 miles

Ⓙ 1500 miles

17. Mary has these coins in a purse. What is the value of the coins?

Ⓐ $0.75

Ⓑ $0.80

Ⓒ $0.90

Ⓓ $1.00

18. Leo started baking potatoes in the oven at 5:45 P.M. He took them out $1\frac{1}{2}$ hours later. Which clock shows the time he took the potatoes out of the oven?

Ⓕ    Ⓗ

Ⓖ 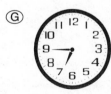   Ⓙ

GO ON ⇨

Practice Test 6 *(continued)*

19. How long is the salamander?
(Use a centimeter ruler.)

Ⓐ 7 cm

Ⓑ 6 cm

Ⓒ 5 cm

Ⓓ 4 cm

20. Timmy has 4 craft sticks. If he lays all
4 sticks end to end, what will be the
total length? (Use an inch ruler.)

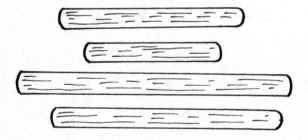

Ⓕ 7 in.

Ⓖ 8 in.

Ⓗ 9 in.

Ⓙ 10 in.

21. A bundle of roof shingles weighs
43 pounds. <u>About</u> how much will
17 bundles weigh?

Ⓐ 400 lb   Ⓒ 800 lb

Ⓑ 600 lb   Ⓓ 1000 lb

Maria went birdwatching on Saturday
and kept track of how many different birds
she saw. Use her tally chart to answer
questions 22 and 23.

Birds Seen

Robins	卌 卌 l
Blue Jays	卌 卌 llll
Sparrows	卌 卌 卌 卌 ll
Thrushes	卌 卌 llll
Warblers	卌 lll

22. How many warblers did Maria see?

Ⓕ 14

Ⓖ 13

Ⓗ 9

Ⓙ 8

23. Maria saw the same number of —

Ⓐ robins and sparrows

Ⓑ blue jays and thrushes

Ⓒ robins and blue jays

Ⓓ thrushes and sparrows

STOP

Practice Test 7

Reading

Directions. Read each sentence and find the meaning of the underlined word. Mark your answer.

1. **The students worked underlined diligently and finished all their work on time. The word diligently means —**
   - Ⓐ carelessly
   - Ⓑ hard
   - Ⓒ slowly
   - Ⓓ alone

2. **Blake used e-mail to transmit a birthday message to his aunt. Transmit means —**
   - Ⓕ remember
   - Ⓖ follow
   - Ⓗ understand
   - Ⓙ send

3. **The pot was so grimy that I had to scrub it twice. Grimy means —**
   - Ⓐ round
   - Ⓑ useful
   - Ⓒ dirty
   - Ⓓ large

4. **The dentist placed some clean implements on a tray beside the patient's chair. The word implements means —**
   - Ⓕ money
   - Ⓖ tools
   - Ⓗ food
   - Ⓙ books

5. **We've been feeding our cat too much, so she has become quite rotund. Rotund means —**
   - Ⓐ friendly
   - Ⓑ healthy
   - Ⓒ nervous
   - Ⓓ plump

6. **When my brother and I squabble, Mom sends us to our rooms. The word squabble means —**
   - Ⓕ practice
   - Ⓖ fight; quarrel
   - Ⓗ exercise
   - Ⓙ help each other

7. **The mayor's bland speech was so boring that I fell asleep. Bland means —**
   - Ⓐ surprising
   - Ⓑ short
   - Ⓒ important
   - Ⓓ dull

8. **Two cars were damaged in the collision, but no one was hurt. Collision means —**
   - Ⓕ crash
   - Ⓖ bridge
   - Ⓗ seat
   - Ⓙ repair

GO ON

Practice Test 7 *(continued)*

Directions. Read each passage. Choose the best answer to each question. Mark your answer.

Decisions, Decisions

At science time, Mr. Felker said, "I've written the names of some rainforest animals on the board. Choose one and write a report about it." While her classmates called out their choices, Tracy thought and thought. She wasn't sure which animal she wanted. She only knew that she *didn't* want to write about a slimy old frog. Then she heard Mr. Felker saying, "So that leaves the frog for Tracy, who hasn't made a choice yet."

At lunch, Tracy pushed her tray through the line. She saw that there were a dozen puddings left but just one cupcake. Tracy thought and thought about which dessert she wanted. Just as she was making up her mind, Seth Graves reached for the cupcake. "I wanted that!" Tracy exclaimed, but Seth just smirked and walked off with the cupcake.

At recess, Heidi Nabors invited Tracy to her house after school. Tracy told Heidi she'd think about it. Then Nina Martinez also invited Tracy over to play. Tracy gave Nina the same answer. Finally Tracy decided she'd go to Heidi's house, but when she told Heidi, she got a big surprise. "Sorry, Tracy," said Heidi. "I just invited Nina to play with me today, and she said yes."

When Dad picked Tracy up after school, he noticed her long face. "Maybe a special dinner will cheer you up," Dad suggested. "Where can I take you tonight?"

This time, Tracy didn't want to miss her chance, so she blurted out, "Let's go to Captain Rick's for hot chicken wings and mashed potatoes!"

With a laugh Dad said, "I admire a young lady who knows exactly what she wants."

9. **Where does this story take place?**
   (A) in a restaurant
   (B) at school
   (C) in a forest
   (D) at Tracy's house

10. **How are Seth and Tracy alike?**
    (F) Both wanted a cupcake.
    (G) Both are friends of Nina.
    (H) Both chose the frogs.
    (J) Both like Captain Rick's.

11. **When Dad picked up Tracy, he "noticed her long face." This means that Tracy looked —**
    (A) silly   (C) unhappy
    (B) surprised   (D) messy

12. **From reading this story, you can tell that Tracy —**
    (F) likes only a few foods
    (G) doesn't like science
    (H) makes some decisions slowly
    (J) doesn't have any friends

GO ON

Practice Test 7 *(continued)*

A Smooth Ride

Maud wasn't looking for a new horse when she rode over to Wilson Ranch, but when she saw Silver galloping around the corral, she knew she wasn't leaving without him. He was strong and swift, and his gray coat shone.

"Sure, you can take him if you can ride him," a cowboy told Maud. "He won't let me near him, and I've given up trying."

Maud took the saddle off her mare and hung it over the fence. Then she walked slowly toward Silver. When he backed away from her, she stood still. Then she started forward again, speaking in a low, soothing voice. "Easy does it, boy." In a few more steps, Maud was beside Silver. She raised her hand to his head and held it there to be sure he wouldn't bolt. Then she gently rubbed the spot between his eyes with her fingertips. Silver nodded his head up and down to encourage her.

The cowboy let out a whistle and said, "You've got a foot in the door now!"

Smiling, Maud picked up her saddle and placed it on Silver's back. Slowly and lightly, she swung herself into the saddle. Silver reared up, and Maud leaned forward and grabbed his bridle. The horse sidestepped left and then right. When he stopped, Maud stroked his neck.

The cowboy pulled off his hat and bowed to Maud. "I wouldn't believe it if I hadn't seen it with my own eyes," he said.

With a laugh, Maud said, "The mare is yours. She's a good work horse." Then she nudged Silver gently with her heels and headed home.

13. Why did Maud want Silver?
- Ⓐ He was strong and beautiful.
- Ⓑ The cowboy was cruel to him.
- Ⓒ Her mare was old and sick.
- Ⓓ She needed two horses.

14. What happened just after Maud rubbed between Silver's eyes?
- Ⓕ Maud put a saddle on Silver.
- Ⓖ Silver backed away from Maud.
- Ⓗ Maud rode away on Silver.
- Ⓙ The cowboy bowed to Maud.

15. What kind of person is Maud?
- Ⓐ patient
- Ⓒ timid
- Ⓑ jolly
- Ⓓ careless

16. The cowboy said, "You've got a foot in the door." He meant that —
- Ⓕ the gate to the corral was open
- Ⓖ it was time for Maud to leave
- Ⓗ Silver was in the barn
- Ⓙ Maud had made a good start

17. When Silver let Maud ride him, the cowboy was —
- Ⓐ frustrated
- Ⓒ amazed
- Ⓑ angry
- Ⓓ embarrassed

Practice Test 7 (continued)

The Fisherman and His Son

One day, a fisherman and his son rowed their boat out to sea. They cast a fishing net into the water and waited for it to fill with fish. Before long, the net was sagging deep in the water. The man and the boy tried to draw it in, but they could not. "The net must be caught on a rock," said the fisherman. "Dive into the water and pull it free."

The boy did as he was told, but in a moment, his head popped out of the water. "The net is caught on an oyster shell that is the size of a boulder!" he shouted. "The shell is open just a crack, and inside is a pearl as big as a coconut!"

"That pearl will make us as rich as kings!" replied the fisherman. "Dive down again and wrap the net around the oyster shell, and then come back to the boat and help me draw it in."

So the boy dove down and wrapped the net around the shell, and then he swam up and climbed into the boat. The fisherman and his son each grabbed a corner of the net and pulled with all their might. Slowly, slowly, they raised the shell out of the water. With their last bit of strength, they yanked the shell into the boat.

The fisherman let out a whoop of joy and exclaimed, "What a treasure we've found!" Then he tried to pry the shell open but could not.

Just then the boat began to take on water. "We're sinking!" cried the boy.

"Jump out of the boat until I can get the pearl free," his father ordered.

Once again, the boy did as he was told. As the fisherman worked to open the shell, the boy swam circles around the boat. He swam ten circles, and then twenty. With each circle, the boy's arms and legs grew heavier, but still his father could not open the shell. Finally, the boy could swim no more. "Father!" he gasped. "Please hurry!"

But the fisherman was thinking only of the pearl, and the boy's cry irritated him. "Be strong! In another minute I will have the pearl."

"Hurry, Father, hurry!" the boy gasped again.

This time the fisherman heard the panic in his son's voice. He looked at the boy and saw how he was struggling. In a minute, he would surely disappear under the water. With the strength of three men, the fisherman seized the shell and tossed it into the water. Then he reached out and grabbed his son's arms and pulled him into the boat.

For a few moments, the fisherman and his son sat in silence. Then the boy finally said, "You must be angry with me, Father."

The fisherman looked at his son and smiled. "I am the happiest man alive," he said, "for what I value most in this world is right here beside me."

GO ON ⇨

Practice Test 7 *(continued)*

18. The fisherman and his son could not draw in their net because it was —

- (F) filled with many pearls
- (G) caught on a rock
- (H) filled with many fish
- (J) caught on an oyster shell

19. The boxes show some things that happened in the story.

1	2	3
The boy wrapped the net around the shell.		The fisherman let out a whoop of joy.

Which of these belongs in Box 2?

- (A) The fisherman and his son rowed their boat out to sea.
- (B) The fisherman tried to pry open the shell.
- (C) The fisherman and his son yanked the shell into the boat.
- (D) The fisherman told his son to be strong.

20. The boat started to sink because —

- (F) a big wave washed over it
- (G) the oyster shell was so heavy
- (H) there was a leak in the bottom
- (J) the boy jumped up and down

21. The story says, "With each circle, the boy's arms and legs grew heavier." What does this mean?

- (A) He had big, strong muscles.
- (B) He was getting tired.
- (C) He was gathering rocks.
- (D) He was gaining weight.

22. How did the fisherman change from the beginning of the story to the end?

- (F) He became a king.
- (G) He stopped being greedy.
- (H) He became old and weak.
- (J) He lost his son's love.

23. What lesson does this story teach?

- (A) A child is a great treasure.
- (B) The sea is full of wonders.
- (C) Hard work always pays off.
- (D) Anyone can become rich.

24. What kind of story is this?

- (F) fairy tale
- (G) biography
- (H) folk tale
- (J) essay

STOP

Practice Test 7

𝔐athematics

Directions. Choose the best answer to each question. Mark your answer. If the correct answer is *not given*, choose "NG."

1. The Jensons are driving from Buffalo to New York City. The distance is 419 miles. They have gone 250 miles so far. How many more miles do they have to go?
   - Ⓐ 159
   - Ⓑ 169
   - Ⓒ 229
   - Ⓓ 669
   - Ⓔ NG

2. A total of 95 students will march in a parade for Memorial Day. They will march in rows of 6 students per row. Which number sentence should you use to find how many rows of students there will be?
   - Ⓕ $95 \div 6 = \square$
   - Ⓖ $95 - 6 = \square$
   - Ⓗ $95 \times 6 = \square$
   - Ⓙ $95 + 6 = \square$
   - Ⓚ NG

3. In one hour, 74 cars went past a tollbooth. The driver of each car paid a $3.00 toll. How much money was collected in all?
   - Ⓐ $77.00
   - Ⓑ $212.00
   - Ⓒ $222.00
   - Ⓓ $252.00
   - Ⓔ NG

4. Jamie made 76 jars of pickles. If he puts 8 jars in a box, how many boxes will he need for 76 jars?
   - Ⓕ 7
   - Ⓖ 8
   - Ⓗ 9
   - Ⓙ 10
   - Ⓚ NG

5. Mrs. Grimes owned 11.6 acres of land. She sold 3.8 acres. How many acres of land does she have left?
   - Ⓐ 6.8
   - Ⓑ 7.3
   - Ⓒ 7.7
   - Ⓓ 8.8
   - Ⓔ NG

GO ON ⇨

Practice Test 7 (continued)

6. Janelle bought this tool kit at a store. She gave the clerk a $20.00 bill.

$15.87

How much change should she receive?

(F) $4.23

(G) $4.13

(H) $4.03

(J) $3.13

(K) NG

7. The table shows the number of children in each grade at the Clark School.

Grade	Number of Children
1	104
2	85
3	92

How many children are there in all?

(A) 270

(B) 271

(C) 280

(D) 291

(E) NG

8. Karen hiked all three trails shown on the map.

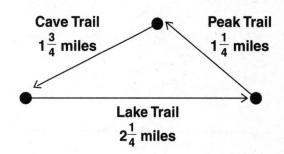

Cave Trail $1\frac{3}{4}$ miles Peak Trail $1\frac{1}{4}$ miles Lake Trail $2\frac{1}{4}$ miles

How far did she hike in all?

(F) $5\frac{1}{4}$ miles

(G) 5 miles

(H) $4\frac{3}{4}$ miles

(J) $4\frac{1}{4}$ miles

(K) NG

9. Drew is 4 feet 4 inches tall. His brother Clancy is 3 feet 9 inches tall. How much taller is Drew?

(A) 3 inches

(B) 4 inches

(C) 5 inches

(D) 7 inches

(E) NG

GO ON

Practice Test 7 *(continued)*

10. A soccer game started at 2:45 P.M. It ended at 4:30 P.M. How long did the game last?
- Ⓕ 1 hr 15 min
- Ⓖ 1 hr 30 min
- Ⓗ 1 hr 45 min
- Ⓙ 2 hr 15 min
- Ⓚ NG

11. Rosa baby-sits for 24 hours each week. She baby-sat for 6 hours on Sunday and 4 hours on Wednesday. How many more hours does she have to baby-sit?
- Ⓐ 14
- Ⓑ 18
- Ⓒ 20
- Ⓓ 34
- Ⓔ NG

12. Liam traveled for 4 weeks and 4 days. How many days is that all together?
- Ⓕ 24
- Ⓖ 28
- Ⓗ 30
- Ⓙ 36
- Ⓚ NG

13. A pea plant is 16 inches tall. It grows 3 inches per week. At this rate, how tall will the plant be in 3 weeks?
- Ⓐ 19 in.
- Ⓑ 22 in.
- Ⓒ 25 in.
- Ⓓ 28 in.
- Ⓔ NG

14. Mike ran 32 miles last week. Shem ran 26 miles. Which number sentence should you use to find how many more miles Mike ran?
- Ⓕ $32 - 26 = \square$
- Ⓖ $32 \div 26 = \square$
- Ⓗ $26 - 32 = \square$
- Ⓙ $26 + 32 = \square$
- Ⓚ NG

15. Lynne started playing basketball at 4:30 P.M. She played for 40 minutes. At what time did she stop playing?
- Ⓐ 5:00 P.M.
- Ⓑ 5:10 P.M.
- Ⓒ 5:20 P.M.
- Ⓓ 5:40 P.M.
- Ⓔ NG

GO ON

Practice Test 7 *(continued)*

16. If you spin this spinner 10 times, which number will the spinner probably land on most often?

Ⓕ 3
Ⓖ 4
Ⓗ 6
Ⓙ 7
Ⓚ NG

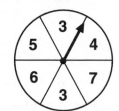

17. A toy store has a large bin of yo-yos. The chart shows how many yo-yos of each color are in the bin.

Color	Number
White	35
Orange	42
Pink	30
Green	54
Black	46

If you reach into the bin without looking and take one yo-yo, which color are you most likely to get?

Ⓐ orange
Ⓑ pink
Ⓒ green
Ⓓ black
Ⓔ NG

18. Mr. Crowley was painting the windows on his house. It took 5 hours to paint 3 windows. At this rate, how long would it take to paint 18 windows?

Ⓕ 21 hours
Ⓖ 24 hours
Ⓗ 27 hours
Ⓙ 30 hours
Ⓚ NG

19. Hannah had $100.00. She spent $64.00 on food and $28.00 for CDs. How much did she have left?

Ⓐ $6.00
Ⓑ $8.00
Ⓒ $18.00
Ⓓ $32.00
Ⓔ NG

20. Steve earned $875 during the summer. Mandy earned $160 more than Steve. How much did Mandy earn?

Ⓕ $715
Ⓖ $935
Ⓗ $985
Ⓙ $1025
Ⓚ NG

GO ON ⇨

Practice Test 7 *(continued)*

21. Stan made a tower of 5 blocks. The yellow block is at the bottom. The red block is between the blue and white blocks. The green block is below the white block but above the yellow block. Which color block is at the top of the tower?

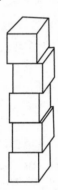

- Ⓐ red
- Ⓑ green
- Ⓒ white
- Ⓓ blue
- Ⓔ NG

22. Amy is making 80 cookies for a bake sale. She made 36 cookies in one batch and 28 cookies in another batch. How many more cookies does she need to make?
- Ⓕ 12
- Ⓖ 16
- Ⓗ 26
- Ⓙ 64
- Ⓚ NG

23. A 4th-grade class went to the Nature Center on a field trip. They spent a total of $124 for tickets. What else do you need to know to figure out how much each ticket cost?
- Ⓐ where the Nature Center was
- Ⓑ what day the trip took place
- Ⓒ the name of the Nature Center
- Ⓓ how many students went on the trip

24. Saul makes $19 an hour at his job. <u>About</u> how much will he earn in 28 hours?
- Ⓕ $30–$40
- Ⓖ $50–$60
- Ⓗ $300–$400
- Ⓙ $500–$600

25. A factory made 1130 brooms on Monday, 2940 brooms on Tuesday, and 1800 brooms on Wednesday. <u>About</u> how many brooms were made in all?
- Ⓐ 8000
- Ⓑ 7000
- Ⓒ 6000
- Ⓓ 5000

STOP

Practice Test 8
Reading

Directions. Choose the word that means the same as the underlined word. Mark your answer.

1. a <u>chilly</u> day
- Ⓐ quiet
- Ⓑ cold
- Ⓒ bright
- Ⓓ tiring

2. with a <u>snarl</u>
- Ⓕ growl
- Ⓖ smile
- Ⓗ wink
- Ⓙ sigh

3. the <u>final</u> chapter
- Ⓐ next
- Ⓑ same
- Ⓒ best
- Ⓓ last

4. cut the <u>cord</u>
- Ⓕ paper
- Ⓖ string
- Ⓗ branch
- Ⓙ cloth

5. the flower's <u>scent</u>
- Ⓐ beauty
- Ⓑ smell
- Ⓒ color
- Ⓓ blossom

Directions. Choose the word that means the **opposite** of the underlined word. Mark your answer.

6. woke up <u>early</u>
- Ⓕ suddenly
- Ⓖ late
- Ⓗ again
- Ⓙ before

7. <u>separated</u> quickly
- Ⓐ left
- Ⓑ interrupted
- Ⓒ joined
- Ⓓ divided

8. a <u>harsh</u> voice
- Ⓕ loud
- Ⓖ distant
- Ⓗ scary
- Ⓙ gentle

9. what was <u>wasted</u>
- Ⓐ saved
- Ⓑ lost
- Ⓒ switched
- Ⓓ grown

10. already <u>melted</u>
- Ⓕ eaten
- Ⓖ gone
- Ⓗ frozen
- Ⓙ shown

Practice Test 8 *(continued)*

Directions. Read each passage. Choose the best answer to each question. Mark your answer.

A Bright Idea

Late one afternoon, 10-year-old Becky Schroeder was sitting in a car while her mother shopped. She thought about using the time to do some homework, but it was getting too dark to see what she was doing. That's when Becky started thinking about a way to make her paper light up so she could write in the dark.

The next day, Becky went to the hardware store and bought a can of phosphorescent paint—the kind that glows in the dark. With the paint and some paper, she shut herself in the bathroom and started experimenting. Becky kept turning the bathroom light on and off as she tested her idea. Finally she came out and said, "It works! I'm writing in the dark!"

Becky's idea became an invention called the Glo-sheet, a clipboard coated with phosphorescent paint. After being exposed to light, the clipboard glows, so it can "light up" a piece of paper placed on top of it. When a newspaper ran a story about the Glo-sheet and the girl who invented it, orders started rolling in from people who need to write in the dark for their jobs and hobbies. That's how young Becky Schoeder became president of the company that makes Glo-sheets.

11. Becky got the idea for her invention when she was —
- Ⓐ sitting in a car
- Ⓑ shopping with her mother
- Ⓒ buying a can of paint
- Ⓓ turning off a light

12. Which detail suggests that many people use Becky's invention?
- Ⓕ "so she could write in the dark"
- Ⓖ "with the paint and some paper"
- Ⓗ "paper placed on top of it"
- Ⓙ "orders started rolling in"

13. A Glo-sheet would probably be most useful for which of these workers?
- Ⓐ a clerk in a store
- Ⓑ a teacher in a classroom
- Ⓒ a scientist in a cave
- Ⓓ a waiter in a restaurant

14. The author of this article probably thinks that —
- Ⓕ everyone needs a Glo-sheet
- Ⓖ Becky is a clever inventor
- Ⓗ the Glo-sheet costs too much
- Ⓙ Becky is too young to have a company

Practice Test 8 *(continued)*

A Few Tips from a Pro

Would you like to be a baby-sitter someday? Mitch Krevans, age 15, has been baby-sitting for four years. Here are Mitch's top five tips.

1. ***Plan ahead.*** I knew the little boy I was baby-sitting loved dinosaurs, so I brought some dinosaur books. Getting the boy to bed was easy because he was excited about his bedtime books. He wanted to go to bed early!

2. ***Never let a child out of your sight.*** I was making lunch in the kitchen for a little girl. She was tumbling in the den and hit her chin on a table. I felt awful because her chin was black and blue when her mom got home.

3. ***Use good sense.*** I baby-sat for twins on a rainy day, and they wanted to play in a mud puddle. "Dad lets us," they said, so I let them. The twins had lots of fun, but their clothes were a mess, and their father wasn't pleased.

4. ***Ask questions.*** When a mom was leaving, I asked for the name and number of her children's doctor. She said, "Now I know my kids are in good hands!" She told other parents about me, and those parents hired me, too.

5. ***Don't take every job.*** I baby-sat one night when I had lots of homework. I made ten dollars, but it wasn't worth it because I had to stay up late to finish my homework.

15. **The main purpose of this article is to —**
   Ⓐ give advice to baby-sitters
   Ⓑ tell funny baby-sitting stories
   Ⓒ describe a bad baby-sitter
   Ⓓ convince kids not to baby-sit

16. **Mitch probably feels worst about the time when —**
   Ⓕ he let twins play in a puddle
   Ⓖ a little girl got hurt
   Ⓗ he had to stay up late
   Ⓙ a boy wanted to go to bed early

17. **Which detail shows that Mitch has baby-sat for several families?**
   Ⓐ "her mother got home"
   Ⓑ "their father wasn't pleased"
   Ⓒ "a mom was leaving"
   Ⓓ "those parents hired me, too"

18. **Mitch asked one mom about the children's doctor because he wanted to —**
   Ⓕ make an appointment for them
   Ⓖ know who to call in an emergency
   Ⓗ ask what the children should eat
   Ⓙ introduce himself to the doctor

19. **Which sentence states an opinion?**
   Ⓐ I brought some dinosaur books.
   Ⓑ I was making lunch.
   Ⓒ I baby-sat for twins on a rainy day.
   Ⓓ I made ten dollars, but it wasn't worth it.

A Handy Experiment

You know you're supposed to wash your hands before you eat, right? Even so, there have probably been times you've skipped the soap and water because your hands looked pretty clean. That's not such a good idea! To find out why, do this fun and easy experiment.

What You Need:

your hand (Don't wash for at least three hours
   before you start the experiment.)
1 teaspoon of beef bouillon powder
1 cup of water
1 package of unflavored gelatin

What You Do: (Ask a grown-up to help you use the stove safely.)

1. Pour the water into a small pot. Heat it until the water is boiling.
2. Add the bouillon powder and gelatin and stir with a mixing spoon until it dissolves.
3. Turn the heat down to low and cover the pot. Continue heating for 30 minutes, stirring occasionally.
4. Pour the liquid into a flat baking dish. Cover and leave for three hours.
5. Remove the dish cover. The gelatin will be firm and a little jiggly. Place your hand on it and press lightly for about 10 seconds.
6. Put the cover on the dish and let it set for three or four days in a warm place.

What Happens Next:

When you uncover the dish after three or four days, prepare to be amazed. You will find a hand-shaped area of gelatin that is covered with small white dots!

Why It Happens:

Your hand is covered with thousands of bacteria that are much too small to see. When you pressed your hand on the gelatin, the bacteria stuck to it. The bacteria grew by using the bouillon as food, and the warmth and dampness of the covered baking dish helped them grow quickly.

So the next time you're tempted to skip the soap and water before a meal, remember how this experiment turned out. In this case, seeing is believing!

GO ON

Practice Test 8 (continued)

20. What is the main idea of this article?

   Ⓕ Bacteria need food to grow.

   Ⓖ Grown-ups can help you do experiments safely.

   Ⓗ Bouillon dissolves in hot water.

   Ⓙ You should wash your hands before you eat.

21. Which sentence states an opinion?

   Ⓐ This experiment is fun and easy to do.

   Ⓑ The gelatin becomes firm and a little jiggly.

   Ⓒ Bacteria on your hand are too small to see.

   Ⓓ Your hand is covered with bacteria.

22. The main purpose of this article is to —

   Ⓕ convince kids to become scientists

   Ⓖ explain how to do an experiment

   Ⓗ tell an entertaining story about cooking

   Ⓙ help kids learn simple cooking skills

23. What is probably the most exciting part of this experiment?

   Ⓐ gathering the materials

   Ⓑ measuring the bouillon and water

   Ⓒ letting the gelatin set for three or four days

   Ⓓ seeing the hand-shaped area covered with white dots

24. This experiment would probably work just as well if you —

   Ⓕ washed your hands right before you started

   Ⓖ left out the bouillon powder

   Ⓗ used a fork for stirring

   Ⓙ let the gelatin set in the refrigerator

25. The white dots you see at the end of this experiment are —

   Ⓐ bits of soap

   Ⓑ groups of bacteria

   Ⓒ pieces of beef

   Ⓓ chunks of gelatin

STOP

Practice Test 8
Mathematics

Directions. Choose the best answer to each question. Mark your answer. If the correct answer is *not given,* choose "NG."

1.

$$195$$
$$76$$
$$+\ 538$$

- (A) 819
- (B) 809
- (C) 808
- (D) 709
- (E) NG

2.

$$304$$
$$-\ 92$$

- (F) 202
- (G) 206
- (H) 212
- (J) 396
- (K) NG

3.

$$571$$
$$-\ 238$$

- (A) 333
- (B) 343
- (C) 347
- (D) 809
- (E) NG

4. This chart shows the number of students who visited the school nurse each day.

Visits to the School Nurse	
Tuesday	11
Wednesday	15
Thursday	16
Friday	18

What was the average number of students who visited the school nurse each day?

- (F) 12
- (G) 14
- (H) 16
- (J) 60
- (K) NG

5. This chart shows the number of people who went to an art show each day.

Day	Number of Visitors
Thursday	271
Friday	328
Saturday	406

How many people went to the art show in all?

- (A) 905
- (B) 995
- (C) 1005
- (D) 1015
- (E) NG

GO ON

Practice Test 8 (continued)

6.
    36
  × 5

(F) 41
(G) 150
(H) 170
(J) 180
(K) NG

7.
    208
  × 4

(A) 872
(B) 832
(C) 632
(D) 212
(E) NG

8.
    70
  × 30

(F) 100
(G) 210
(H) 2100
(J) 2900
(K) NG

9. 7 × □ = 42

(A) 5
(B) 7
(C) 8
(D) 9
(E) NG

10. Pilar has 3 different colored skirts and 5 different blouses.

3   5

How many different combinations of one skirt and one blouse can she make?

(F) 8
(G) 10
(H) 15
(J) 16
(K) NG

11. Cal has these loose socks in a drawer.

Color	Number
Blue	6
White	7
Brown	8
Black	3

If Cal takes one sock out of the drawer without looking, what is the probability that he will get a brown sock?

(A) $\frac{1}{3}$

(B) $\frac{1}{24}$

(C) $\frac{1}{4}$

(D) $\frac{1}{6}$

(E) NG

GO ON

Practice Test 8 *(continued)*

12. $36 \div 4 =$

 Ⓕ 6
 Ⓖ 7
 Ⓗ 8
 Ⓙ 9
 Ⓚ NG

13. $8\overline{)64}$

 Ⓐ 6
 Ⓑ 7
 Ⓒ 8
 Ⓓ 9
 Ⓔ NG

14. $3\overline{)96}$

 Ⓕ 30
 Ⓖ 31
 Ⓗ 33
 Ⓙ 320
 Ⓚ NG

15. $4\overline{)800}$

 Ⓐ 240
 Ⓑ 220
 Ⓒ 210
 Ⓓ 22
 Ⓔ NG

16. The grid map shows where five towns are located.

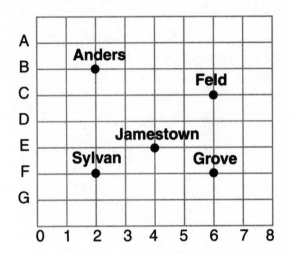

Which town is located at 4E?

 Ⓕ Jamestown
 Ⓖ Anders
 Ⓗ Grove
 Ⓙ Sylvan
 Ⓚ NG

17. Mr. Graves wrote this number sentence on the blackboard.

$$(12 + n) - 8 = 20$$

What is the value of *n?*

 Ⓐ 4
 Ⓑ 12
 Ⓒ 16
 Ⓓ 28
 Ⓔ NG

GO ON ▶

Practice Test 8 (continued)

18. This chart lists the number of cars sold by Auto Shop in each of 4 months.

Vehicles Sold	
May	12
June	10
July	16
August	14

What was the average number of cars sold per month?

(F) 52

(G) 14

(H) 13

(J) 12

(K) NG

19. Leanne wrote this number sentence to solve a problem.

$(6 \times n) - 10 = 20$

What is the value of n?

(A) 30

(B) 8

(C) 6

(D) 5

(E) NG

The grid below shows the location of five points. Use the grid to answer questions 20 and 21.

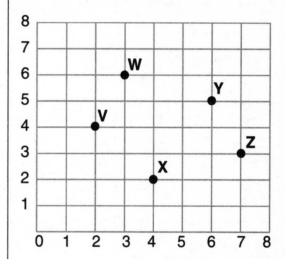

20. What point is located at (4, 2)?

(F) W

(G) X

(H) Y

(J) Z

(K) NG

21. What is the location of point Y?

(A) (5, 6)

(B) (7, 3)

(C) (2, 4)

(D) (3, 6)

(E) NG

GO ON

Practice Test 8 (continued)

22. $\frac{3}{10} + \frac{9}{10} =$

Ⓕ $\frac{10}{12}$

Ⓖ $\frac{12}{20}$

Ⓗ $\frac{3}{5}$

Ⓙ $1\frac{1}{5}$

Ⓚ NG

23. $\frac{5}{8}$
$+ \frac{3}{8}$

Ⓐ $\frac{1}{4}$

Ⓑ $\frac{7}{8}$

Ⓒ $\frac{3}{4}$

Ⓓ 1

Ⓔ NG

24. $\frac{5}{9}$
$- \frac{4}{9}$

Ⓕ $\frac{1}{9}$

Ⓖ $\frac{9}{18}$

Ⓗ $\frac{1}{4}$

Ⓙ 1

Ⓚ NG

25. $6.3 + 4.5 =$

Ⓐ 1.8

Ⓑ 10.2

Ⓒ 10.6

Ⓓ 11.8

Ⓔ NG

26. $14.85 + 7.7 =$

Ⓕ 23.55

Ⓖ 22.55

Ⓗ 22.25

Ⓙ 7.15

Ⓚ NG

27. $28.50
       - 19.95$

Ⓐ $8.55

Ⓑ $11.45

Ⓒ $18.55

Ⓓ $48.45

Ⓔ NG

28. $26.04 - 18.9 =$

Ⓕ 7.05

Ⓖ 7.14

Ⓗ 8.5

Ⓙ 44.94

Ⓚ NG

STOP

ANSWER SHEET

Practice Test # _____

Student Name _____ Grade _____

Teacher Name _____ Date _____

READING		MATHEMATICS	

READING

1 Ⓐ Ⓑ Ⓒ Ⓓ	21 Ⓐ Ⓑ Ⓒ Ⓓ	1 Ⓐ Ⓑ Ⓒ Ⓓ Ⓔ	21 Ⓐ Ⓑ Ⓒ Ⓓ Ⓔ
2 Ⓕ Ⓖ Ⓗ Ⓙ	22 Ⓕ Ⓖ Ⓗ Ⓙ	2 Ⓕ Ⓖ Ⓗ Ⓙ Ⓚ	22 Ⓕ Ⓖ Ⓗ Ⓙ Ⓚ
3 Ⓐ Ⓑ Ⓒ Ⓓ	23 Ⓐ Ⓑ Ⓒ Ⓓ	3 Ⓐ Ⓑ Ⓒ Ⓓ Ⓔ	23 Ⓐ Ⓑ Ⓒ Ⓓ Ⓔ
4 Ⓕ Ⓖ Ⓗ Ⓙ	24 Ⓕ Ⓖ Ⓗ Ⓙ	4 Ⓕ Ⓖ Ⓗ Ⓙ Ⓚ	24 Ⓕ Ⓖ Ⓗ Ⓙ Ⓚ
5 Ⓐ Ⓑ Ⓒ Ⓓ	25 Ⓐ Ⓑ Ⓒ Ⓓ	5 Ⓐ Ⓑ Ⓒ Ⓓ Ⓔ	25 Ⓐ Ⓑ Ⓒ Ⓓ Ⓔ
6 Ⓕ Ⓖ Ⓗ Ⓙ	26 Ⓕ Ⓖ Ⓗ Ⓙ	6 Ⓕ Ⓖ Ⓗ Ⓙ Ⓚ	26 Ⓕ Ⓖ Ⓗ Ⓙ Ⓚ
7 Ⓐ Ⓑ Ⓒ Ⓓ	27 Ⓐ Ⓑ Ⓒ Ⓓ	7 Ⓐ Ⓑ Ⓒ Ⓓ Ⓔ	27 Ⓐ Ⓑ Ⓒ Ⓓ Ⓔ
8 Ⓕ Ⓖ Ⓗ Ⓙ	28 Ⓕ Ⓖ Ⓗ Ⓙ	8 Ⓕ Ⓖ Ⓗ Ⓙ Ⓚ	28 Ⓕ Ⓖ Ⓗ Ⓙ Ⓚ
9 Ⓐ Ⓑ Ⓒ Ⓓ	29 Ⓐ Ⓑ Ⓒ Ⓓ	9 Ⓐ Ⓑ Ⓒ Ⓓ Ⓔ	29 Ⓐ Ⓑ Ⓒ Ⓓ Ⓔ
10 Ⓕ Ⓖ Ⓗ Ⓙ	30 Ⓕ Ⓖ Ⓗ Ⓙ	10 Ⓕ Ⓖ Ⓗ Ⓙ Ⓚ	30 Ⓕ Ⓖ Ⓗ Ⓙ Ⓚ
11 Ⓐ Ⓑ Ⓒ Ⓓ	31 Ⓐ Ⓑ Ⓒ Ⓓ	11 Ⓐ Ⓑ Ⓒ Ⓓ Ⓔ	31 Ⓐ Ⓑ Ⓒ Ⓓ Ⓔ
12 Ⓕ Ⓖ Ⓗ Ⓙ	32 Ⓕ Ⓖ Ⓗ Ⓙ	12 Ⓕ Ⓖ Ⓗ Ⓙ Ⓚ	32 Ⓕ Ⓖ Ⓗ Ⓙ Ⓚ
13 Ⓐ Ⓑ Ⓒ Ⓓ	33 Ⓐ Ⓑ Ⓒ Ⓓ	13 Ⓐ Ⓑ Ⓒ Ⓓ Ⓔ	33 Ⓐ Ⓑ Ⓒ Ⓓ Ⓔ
14 Ⓕ Ⓖ Ⓗ Ⓙ	34 Ⓕ Ⓖ Ⓗ Ⓙ	14 Ⓕ Ⓖ Ⓗ Ⓙ Ⓚ	34 Ⓕ Ⓖ Ⓗ Ⓙ Ⓚ
15 Ⓐ Ⓑ Ⓒ Ⓓ	35 Ⓐ Ⓑ Ⓒ Ⓓ	15 Ⓐ Ⓑ Ⓒ Ⓓ Ⓔ	35 Ⓐ Ⓑ Ⓒ Ⓓ Ⓔ
16 Ⓕ Ⓖ Ⓗ Ⓙ	36 Ⓕ Ⓖ Ⓗ Ⓙ	16 Ⓕ Ⓖ Ⓗ Ⓙ Ⓚ	36 Ⓕ Ⓖ Ⓗ Ⓙ Ⓚ
17 Ⓐ Ⓑ Ⓒ Ⓓ	37 Ⓐ Ⓑ Ⓒ Ⓓ	17 Ⓐ Ⓑ Ⓒ Ⓓ Ⓔ	37 Ⓐ Ⓑ Ⓒ Ⓓ Ⓔ
18 Ⓕ Ⓖ Ⓗ Ⓙ	38 Ⓕ Ⓖ Ⓗ Ⓙ	18 Ⓕ Ⓖ Ⓗ Ⓙ Ⓚ	38 Ⓕ Ⓖ Ⓗ Ⓙ Ⓚ
19 Ⓐ Ⓑ Ⓒ Ⓓ	39 Ⓐ Ⓑ Ⓒ Ⓓ	19 Ⓐ Ⓑ Ⓒ Ⓓ Ⓔ	39 Ⓐ Ⓑ Ⓒ Ⓓ Ⓔ
20 Ⓕ Ⓖ Ⓗ Ⓙ	40 Ⓕ Ⓖ Ⓗ Ⓙ	20 Ⓕ Ⓖ Ⓗ Ⓙ Ⓚ	40 Ⓕ Ⓖ Ⓗ Ⓙ Ⓚ

Practice Test 1

Tested Skills	Item Numbers
READING (1–26)	
Vocabulary	
Identify word meaning	1–12
Comprehension	
Sequence	14, 22
Make predictions	13, 21
Make inferences	19, 23
Character	15, 18, 25
Literary elements (setting, plot, mood, genre, theme)	16, 17, 26
Make judgments	20, 24
MATHEMATICS (1–28)	
Numeration and Number Concepts	
Associate numerals and number words	1, 19
Compare and order whole numbers	3, 10, 11
Use place value and rounding	5, 12, 13, 21, 22
Identify number patterns	7, 9, 17, 20
Estimation	15, 23
Factoring	18
Identify fractional parts	4, 8, 28
Compare and order fractions	6, 27
Apply operational properties (zero, addition/subtraction, commutative property)	2, 14, 16, 24, 25, 26

Practice Test 2

Tested Skills	Item Numbers
READING (1–22)	
Vocabulary	
Multiple-meaning words	1–6
Comprehension	
Context clues	7, 14, 21
Cause and effect	12, 17
Draw conclusions	15, 19
Main idea and supporting details	10, 11, 16, 20
Comparison/contrast	8, 13, 18
Fact/opinion	9, 22
MATHEMATICS (1–22)	
Geometry and Measurement	
Identify plane and solid figures and their parts	1, 2
Recognize symmetry and congruence	5
Identify lines (intersecting, parallel)	3, 4
Identify transformations	6
Find perimeter and area	7, 8
Recognize money	9
Tell time	10, 11
Identify appropriate units of measurement	12, 13
Use measurement instruments (rulers, thermometer)	14, 15, 16
Estimate measurements	17, 18
Interpret bar graphs, tables, charts	19, 20, 21, 22

Practice Test 3

Tested Skills	Item Numbers

READING (1–22)
Vocabulary
  Context clues
Comprehension
  Sequence
  Make predictions
  Make inferences
  Character
  Form generalizations
  Literary elements (setting, plot, mood, genre, theme)
	
	1–8
	
	14, 18
	10, 17
	9, 19
	11, 15
	12, 21, 22
	13, 16, 20

MATHEMATICS (1–25)
Problem Solving
  Solve one-step problems using basic operations
  Solve problems involving money, time, measurement
  Solve problems involving estimation and ratio/proportion
  Solve problems involving probability and logic
  Identify steps in solving problems
  Solve multi-step problems
	
	1, 3, 4, 5, 8, 24
	6, 7, 9, 11, 12, 15
	13, 18, 21, 22
	16, 17, 19
	2, 14, 23
	10, 20, 25

Practice Test 4

Tested Skills	Item Numbers

READING (1–25)
Vocabulary
  Synonyms and antonyms
Comprehension
  Cause and effect
  Draw conclusions
  Main idea and supporting details
  Author's purpose and point of view
  Fact/opinion
  Evaluate evidence to support ideas
	
	1–10
	
	19, 24
	14, 17, 18, 21
	11, 12
	15, 20, 25
	16, 22
	13, 23

MATHEMATICS (1–28)
Computation
  Add and subtract whole numbers
  Multiply whole numbers
  Divide whole numbers
  Add and subtract fractions
  Add and subtract decimals
  Find average, probability, and combinations
  Solve simple equations
  Find coordinates on a grid
	
	1, 2, 3, 5
	6, 7, 8, 9
	12, 13, 14, 15
	22, 23, 24
	25, 26, 27, 28
	4, 10, 11, 18
	17, 19
	16, 20, 21

Practice Test 5

Tested Skills	Item Numbers
READING (1–28)	
Vocabulary	
Identify word meaning	1–12
Comprehension	
Figurative language	13, 21, 23
Cause and effect	15, 19, 22
Make inferences	18, 20, 26
Character	14, 24
Comparison/contrast	17, 27
Literary elements (setting, plot, mood, genre, theme)	16, 25, 28
MATHEMATICS (1–28)	
Numeration and Number Concepts	
Associate numerals and number words	1, 19
Compare and order whole numbers	3, 10, 11
Use place value and rounding	5, 12, 13, 21, 22
Identify patterns	7, 9, 17, 20
Estimation	15, 23
Factoring	18, 25
Identify fractional parts	4, 8, 26
Compare and order fractions	6, 27
Apply operational properties (zero, addition/subtraction, commutative property)	2, 14, 16, 24, 28

Practice Test 6

Tested Skills	Item Numbers
READING (1–22)	
Vocabulary	
Multiple-meaning words	1–6
Comprehension	
Context clues	7, 12, 17
Draw conclusions	10, 13, 18
Main idea and supporting details	11, 16, 20
Form generalizations	8, 19
Author's purpose and point of view	15, 21, 22
Make judgments	9, 14
MATHEMATICS (1–23)	
Geometry and Measurement	
Identify plane and solid figures and their parts	1, 2, 3
Recognize symmetry and congruence	4, 9
Identify lines (intersecting, parallel)	5, 6
Identify transformations	12
Find perimeter and area	10, 14
Recognize money	17
Tell time	13, 18
Identify appropriate units of measurement	11, 15
Use measurement instruments	19, 20
Estimate measurements	16, 21
Interpret bar graphs, tables, charts	7, 8, 22, 23

Practice Test 7

Tested Skills	Item Numbers
READING (1–24)	
Vocabulary	
Context clues	1–8
Comprehension	
Figurative language	11, 16, 21
Cause and effect	13, 18, 20
Sequence	14, 19
Character	12, 15, 17
Comparison/contrast	10, 22
Literary elements (setting, plot, mood, genre, theme)	9, 23, 24
MATHEMATICS (1–25)	
Problem Solving	
Solve one-step problems using basic operations	1, 3, 4, 5, 7, 20
Solve problems involving money, time, measurement	6, 8, 9, 10, 12, 15
Solve problems involving estimation and ratio/proportion	13, 18, 24, 25
Solve problems involving probability and logic	16, 17, 21
Identify steps in solving problems	2, 14, 23
Solve multi-step problems	11, 19, 22

Practice Test 8

Tested Skills	Item Numbers
READING (1–25)	
Vocabulary	
Synonyms and antonyms	1–10
Comprehension	
Make inferences	18, 24, 25
Main idea and supporting details	11, 20
Author's purpose and point of view	14, 15, 22
Make judgments	13, 16, 23
Fact/opinion	19, 21
Evaluate evidence to support ideas	12, 17
MATHEMATICS (1–28)	
Computation	
Add and subtract whole numbers	1, 2, 3, 5
Multiply whole numbers	6, 7, 8, 9
Divide whole numbers	12, 13, 14, 15
Add and subtract fractions	22, 23, 24
Add and subtract decimals	25, 26, 27, 28
Find average, probability, and combinations	4, 10, 11, 18
Solve simple equations	17, 19
Find coordinates on a grid	16, 20, 21

ANSWER KEY

Practice Test 1

READING
Vocabulary
1. B
2. J
3. D
4. G
5. C
6. F
7. C
8. F
9. C
10. F
11. B
12. J

Comprehension
13. D
14. F
15. B
16. H
17. C
18. J
19. C
20. H
21. D
22. F
23. D
24. J
25. C
26. G

MATHEMATICS
Numeration and Number Concepts
1. C
2. G
3. B
4. J
5. C
6. J
7. D
8. F
9. B
10. J
11. A
12. G
13. C
14. H
15. D
16. F
17. B
18. H
19. A
20. J
21. B
22. G
23. D
24. J
25. B
26. H
27. B
28. F

Practice Test 2

READING
Vocabulary
1. A
2. G
3. C
4. G
5. C
6. J

Comprehension
7. B
8. J
9. C
10. F
11. B
12. H
13. C
14. F
15. D
16. G
17. D
18. F
19. A
20. J
21. C
22. G

MATHEMATICS
Geometry and Measurement
1. C
2. G
3. B
4. F
5. D
6. H
7. B
8. H
9. D
10. J
11. C
12. G
13. A
14. J
15. C
16. H
17. D
18. G
19. C
20. G
21. D
22. F

ANSWER KEY

Practice Test 3

READING
Vocabulary
1. D
2. F
3. D
4. H
5. A
6. H
7. B
8. G

Comprehension
9. B
10. J
11. C
12. H
13. C
14. F
15. B
16. H
17. C
18. G
19. D
20. G
21. D
22. F

MATHEMATICS
Problem Solving
1. B
2. J
3. C
4. H
5. E
6. G
7. E
8. J
9. C
10. J
11. B
12. H
13. D
14. K
15. D
16. F
17. C
18. J
19. A
20. F
21. C
22. H
23. A
24. G
25. B

Practice Test 4

READING
Vocabulary
1. A
2. J
3. B
4. G
5. C
6. G
7. A
8. J
9. C
10. G

Comprehension
11. D
12. G
13. A
14. H
15. A
16. H
17. B
18. F
19. D
20. G
21. D
22. F
23. C
24. J
25. A

MATHEMATICS
Computation
1. D
2. K
3. C
4. G
5. B
6. J
7. E
8. H
9. C
10. G
11. A
12. K
13. C
14. G
15. D
16. J
17. A
18. H
19. E
20. G
21. D
22. H
23. A
24. G
25. B
26. K
27. D
28. J

ANSWER KEY

Practice Test 5

READING
Vocabulary
1. B
2. F
3. C
4. J
5. C
6. G
7. A
8. H
9. D
10. F
11. B
12. J

Comprehension
13. B
14. H
15. D
16. F
17. B
18. H
19. A
20. G
21. A
22. F
23. C
24. G
25. D
26. J
27. A
28. H

MATHEMATICS
Numeration and Number Concepts
1. B
2. F
3. D
4. H
5. C
6. G
7. A
8. J
9. C
10. G
11. D
12. H
13. C
14. J
15. D
16. G
17. B
18. F
19. B
20. H
21. D
22. H
23. C
24. F
25. A
26. G
27. A
28. J

Practice Test 6

READING
Vocabulary
1. D
2. H
3. A
4. H
5. B
6. G

Comprehension
7. C
8. G
9. D
10. G
11. B
12. H
13. A
14. J
15. C
16. F
17. B
18. J
19. A
20. J
21. B
22. H

MATHEMATICS
Geometry and Measurement
1. B
2. J
3. A
4. F
5. B
6. H
7. C
8. H
9. A
10. G
11. D
12. J
13. C
14. J
15. B
16. H
17. D
18. F
19. A
20. H
21. C
22. J
23. B

ANSWER KEY

Practice Test 7

READING
Vocabulary
1. B
2. J
3. C
4. G
5. D
6. G
7. D
8. F

Comprehension
9. B
10. F
11. C
12. H
13. A
14. F
15. A
16. J
17. C
18. J
19. C
20 G
21. B
22. G
23. A
24. H

MATHEMATICS
Problem Solving
1. B
2. F
3. C
4. J
5. E
6. G
7. E
8. F
9. D
10. H
11. A
12. K
13. C
14. F
15. B
16. F
17. C
18. J
19. B
20. K
21. D
22. G
23. D
24. J
25. C

Practice Test 8

READING
Vocabulary
1. B
2. F
3. D
4. G
5. B
6. G
7. C
8. J
9. A
10. H

Comprehension
11. A
12. J
13. C
14. G
15. A
16. G
17. D
18. G
19. D
20. J
21. A
22. G
23. D
24. H
25. B

MATHEMATICS
Computation
1. B
2. H
3. A
4. K
5. C
6. J
7. B
8. H
9. E
10. H
11. A
12. J
13. C
14. K
15. E
16. F
17. C
18. H
19. D
20. G
21. E
22. J
23. D
24. F
25. E
26. G
27. A
28. G